Hannah Böggeln

To believe in Jesus

To Believe in Jesus

Ruth Burrows

DIMENSION BOOKS
DENVILLE, NEW JERSEY 07834

To Father, Jo and Rita
to Ann
and those whom they represent for me

As always, I am indebted to W.

DIMENSION BOOKS
Denville, New Jersey

FIRST AMERICAN EDITION   1981

0-87193-154-0

Contents

Introduction

Up to now I had resisted the pressure put upon me by my friends to write another book. I felt I had said all I needed to say in *Before the Living God* and *Guidelines for Mystical Prayer* and did not want to write for the sake of writing. What has helped to change my mind is the fact that though I expressly state that *Guidelines for Mystical Prayer* is intended for lay people every bit as much as for religious, many lay people – especially the ones who could most profit from it – instinctively feel it is not for them. It is too specialised. Could I not spell out the message with them more precisely in mind?

For me, there is simply no distinction to be made between lay people and religious when we are speaking of spiritual growth. It is the same for each and all. Yet I fear that, in spite of lip service being paid to this equality, the majority of lay people and religious at least secretly assume a huge distinction. On the part of religious I have nothing to say save that it argues to a blindness and conceitedness, as well as to a misunderstanding of God and his workings, which put a stop to all real growth. On the part of lay people, it may seem like humility but it is not so. It shows a lack of trust in God and also a lack of generosity. The conviction that we are not called to the same high state as are religious, that we have not received equal grace and favour, serves as a useful alibi for not trying with all our heart. If we were convinced, as we should be, that our grace and calling in no way falls behind that of religious, that the call to total holiness is for us too, then nothing can excuse us from effort.

Again, it is said that I take so much for granted in *Guidelines for Mystical Prayer* and this, I realise, is true. As the wisest of the wise has remarked, the number of those to whom the second half of the book applies is small, yet it is these later chapters that have been more drawn out. What is needed is to help people to live in such a way that secretly, unknown to themselves, God will be leading them further, taking them into his mystery. That argument makes sense to me. It is only in the first stages that we really need guidance. Once we have been drawn into the luminous darkness which is Jesus, he is our light. We will never be able to take stock and say : 'Now I am past the first stages and what is said there does not apply to me any more'. One truly in the mystical dimension, and anyone familiar with *Guidelines for Mystical Prayer* will understand what I mean by the term, will peacefully assume that he is only in the first stages and will go on labouring to do those things he has been trying for all along – to be loving and unselfish, faithful to his duties, not bothering where he is on the map. It does no one any harm to think he is less advanced than in fact he is, but it does him immeasurable harm to assume he is further on than really is so.

What more than anything else has broken my resistance to writing is the knowledge that often enough both *Before the Living God* and *Guidelines for Mystical Prayer* have been misinterpreted, even by those who express appreciation of them, religious as well as lay people. Further, questions have been raised in regard to them which have forced me to try other ways of expressing what is in my mind. Inevitably insight has grown and greater clarity of thought. I do not think anything will be added to what is in the other two books but maybe at least for some I can achieve a more lucid expression of my ideas.

Then there is the concern I feel at many current notions about prayer and spiritual growth. Humanly speaking I feel reluctant to appear critical of what is called the modern interest in prayer and of the many books catering for this avid interest.

How could one not applaud any movement which even remotely might lead people to deeper faith? I certainly do applaud. It is the same with regard to certain books. Often they are the fruit of great compassion and contain many excellent, helpful things, but I feel there is often an underlying confusion, if not error, which will ultimately lead to sterility in spite of temporary enthusiasm and impressive first fruits. In vain I look for the one essential element in all truly christian prayer, namely a deep, all-pervading grasp of the mediatorship of Jesus, in other words, real faith in Jesus. The pages that follow will be an attempt to draw out what faith in Jesus really means, how rare it is, how it is acquired, how it grows and eventually flowers in perfect union or transformation into him.

It is with delight and relief that I am relying on one authority only, that of scripture. It was by way of scripture that I came myself to understand what I do. It was only much later on that I began to see what the great mystical writers were saying and that it was the same as the scriptures said. Hitherto much of what they said had been closed to me and unattractive, whereas scripture was always eloquent. It seems to me this is as it should be and the only safe way. I think that mystical writers of the past can easily be misunderstood, and wrong conclusions drawn from them to the detriment of our progress in the love of God.

I shall be forced back on theory. I wish it were not so, and indeed it would be unnecessary were we not already imbued with many wrong theories. Some of the readers of *Guidelines for Mystical Prayer* expressed dislike of the division of the spiritual journey into three stages. To some it would be wisest to say they had best ignore it and just go on with living; they do not need to advert to it. But to others might not the relevant answer be that perhaps they need to know it so as to shake their complacency? Perhaps their dislike of such divisions derives from the fear of being shown they are not far on the path. When no distinctions are made and outlines left blurred they could perhaps live with their illusions. Yet such fears are indicative of the very thing we must always be pointing out, namely that we are seeking ourselves and not God. If we really want God then we are all eagerness to know the truth about ourselves, to be told we are moving in the wrong direction and need to be put right. If we are wanting ourselves we hate and resent having misgivings aroused.

If we could start from scratch, with no preconceived notions of the route, and if our hearts were firmly fixed on our journey's end, with gospel in hand we would have no further need of route marking, no need of signposts. Jesus himself, through his Holy Spirit, would guide our hearts aright. And even now I am convinced that anyone who truly seeks God rather than himself will find him, and this in spite of being directed into wrong paths. The Holy Spirit will lead him, secretly, probably painfully but most surely.

The trouble is so very few of us really do seek God. We want something for ourselves and this is why we are anxious to be told the way. We want the path marked out for us, securely walled in, with not a chance of going astray. We are so anxious for this that we cannot afford to listen to the Lord guiding us from within. If we did listen then we would realise that we were merely going round in circles within the given confines, and that if we would find God we must venture out into the trackless, unknown wastes. Whilst we are busy circuiting the well-worn track described for us by others, we cannot conceive what it is like outside, or even that there is one. So to some extent sign-post must replace sign-post. On each sign-post one word only will be written, however; the name of Jesus, for he alone is the way, there is no other.

Finally, I want to convince anyone who reads these pages that God's call is to him, that God offers him the closest union. This is not the prerogative of a few privileged persons, it is his birthright. Nothing can excuse him from failing to attain it. To be a christian means to be called to total holiness. On the other hand it must be pointed out that, though it is the common heritage, it is not commonly attained. Too easily we speak of a man or woman being holy, a saint and so forth. Any close look at the one in question would reveal areas of selfishness and pride which are incompatible with true holiness. We must not use the word glibly; we must have a true notion of christian holiness and set our standard high. Yet it won't be a standard of mere virtue – that can be high without holiness – but one of love and of humility, and surrender to our Lord.

Nothing extraordinary is demanded; no situation is, of itself, inhibitive. Someone who had read and was moved by *Guidelines for Mystical Prayer* wrote telling me of his impressions. He ended rather sadly by saying that the way was not for him, he was already settled in his life's role – he was a family man – and there was no possibility of changing it. What a wholly wrong interpretation. God could not be asking him to change his way of life. I cannot escape the thought that this sort of thing is an excuse. He had glimpsed something of the deep self-denial demanded, could not face it, and explained it away to himself in this manner. There is a price to be paid but it is within everyone's grasp. It is simply this, we must trust Jesus to such an extent that we hand ourself over to him.

What I am saying in these writings will not be popular, but then our Lord's teaching was not popular. People were entranced by his lovely personality, his magnetism, his power over sickness, and the sense of hope he inspired. Allured by these they followed him and listened. But when the implications of what he was teaching began to dawn upon them they went away and walked no more with him. He did not answer their expectations and in their bitter disillusionment they were willing to throw him to the lions. The religious leaders hounded him to death. Only those who knew their need of God and humbly accepted living with that need found deep, overwhelming joy in the message he gave, a message only the humble can receive, one which the pride of man, the primal pride which is basic to us all, finds revolting.

I

Do you believe in the Son of Man?

Do you believe in the Son of Man? To this question addressed by Jesus to the man he had cured of blindness I am sure each of us would reply with a hearty 'yes'. We would be sincere, but we would not be speaking the truth. Faith in Jesus, the Son of Man, is very, very rare. If what I say is true it is a depressing assertion. It would be even more depressing if there were nothing we could do about it. As it is, we are set over a gold mine, a shovel is put in our hands, we are given the strength to dig and the absolute assurance that if we do so we shall find. No special gifts are required, no superhuman effort, only resolution and the taking of trouble. Everyone is given the chance, no one is excluded. What happens? Some of us at any rate set to work and dig but what we find is not at all what we expected. We expected a glistening nugget and instead all we have in our weary hands is an ugly, shapeless lump of metal. 'It is gold, pure gold,' we are told. But it doesn't look like gold, it doesn't feel like gold. You say you believe in Jesus. He told you that if you dug you would find the treasure. Where is your faith?

Faith is a gift but a gift that will undoubtedly be given if we take the necessary steps and choose to believe, choose to take God at his word and stake our lives on it. He has told us, through Jesus, that he loves us, that he will do everything for us; he has assured us that when we ask we receive, that when we seek we find, that when we knock the door is opened. Do we take him at his word? What we receive, what we find, whither we are led doesn't seem to be God. The treasure doesn't seem treasure but dross. Deepest challenge of faith at the very outset! Do you believe in the Son of Man? God comes to us in the lowly man of Nazareth, in what does not flatter our pride but humbles it to the dust. Where God truly is there man must in consequence feel he 'is not', naught. Isaiah graphically described the perennial truth that men turn away in revulsion from the face of God revealed in his suffering servant.

When we come to the spiritual life, when we bend ourselves to prayer, as often as not what we are wanting is that it will make us feel good, that it will change the whole feel of our life and that an aura will be cast over us and all around us. This does not happen. On the contrary we are likely to feel even less colourful than before. Can we take this? We haven't any alternative of course but we can find ways of mitigating this sense of failure, this bitter disappointment of our expectations. But if we have faith we are not disappointed, not deceived. We recognise treasure in the dross because we know God is faithful and never disappoints. We are able to recognise the face of God in the marred face of Jesus. Whatever we feel or don't feel we are certain that our prayer is heard, that our desires are or will be fulfilled. We do not ask to have the proof of this in our hand, we want no assurance other than the one absolute assurance which is always to be had: God has given us his word, Jesus has said so. 'Have you believed because you have seen me? Blessed are those who have not seen and yet believe' (Jn 20 : 29). If we believe in Jesus we are happy to go on without any evidence, without feedback, praying into the void, unwaveringly certain. But are we like this? Don't we crave some assurance from within our own experience, something to show for our effort? Faith asks for none.

In this first chapter I wanted to show straight away that to say we have little or no faith in Jesus is not shock tactics but a simple statement of fact. Yet this is only to scratch the surface. The more we go on thinking about it, being honest with ourselves, the more we shall see the truth of the statement. Here, at the outset, I have indicated the mortal enemy of faith – our own selfishness. It is one thing to give an intellectual assent to the truth of Jesus and to his role in our lives, quite another to believe in him, or on him, as an older translation aptly has it – that is, make him and him alone the ground on which we stand, the vantage point from which we view all things, make all judgments and choices. True faith is not a mere assent of the mind leaving the rest of us untouched, it is a sword penetrating our inmost vitals, leaving no area unaffected. It is no wonder we are not in a hurry to believe. It is going to mean the destruction of self-seeking. Over and over again we must realise how, in what we think of as our love and service of God, lurks a ravenous self-seeking which would use God to inflate self. True faith destroys this enemy.

For many of us, faith means little more than an assent to a whole range of dogmas which, we are told, God has revealed. Loyalty to God and worship of him demand this assent. That we should see relevance in these dogmas, that they should enter intimately into our lives and exist for that very purpose, does not seem to matter. They are over there, our living is here, and there is no real connection between the two. Of course we must lead a good life, that is taken for granted, but we do not see the connection between believing dogmas and living as a christian. What is true of the poorly instructed is just as likely to be true of the sophisticated. Even with a great weight of theology on our back there can still be a divorce between what we assent to with our mind and how we live. Now this is wrong. What God reveals is for living and only for living, not to adorn books or cultivate the human mind. What God reveals is himself, as a lover reveals himself to the beloved. God summons us to a love relationship and this summons of love demands a response of our whole person in the whole of our living. Human life has no other meaning than to be a response to the God who calls us to love.

Faith covers every aspect of our relation to God in our earthly existence : from its beginning, which is the grace to accept Jesus of Nazareth as God's messenger, to that encounter with him which must surely come if we are faithful, an encounter which means a going down with him into death, in order to rise with him in perfect fulfilment when, still in this world, 'I lay hold of that for which Christ has laid hold of me'. If the essence of the divine goal is an embrace of love, faith is the arms with which we enfold our beloved.

Faith is inseparable from love. This is clearly seen in human relationships and these are our best analogy precisely because God has revealed himself in our human terms and revealed himself as lover. We know how wide-ranging can be the degrees of faith we have in a person. An employer can trust his employee. He can rely on him to be honest, hard working, thrifty. A man can trust his associates and friends to deal fairly with him, protect his good name and be concerned with all that concerns him. But there is probably one whom he can trust above all others, in whom he can believe to such an extent that he can place his life in her hands.

All really deep relationships are going to demand at some stage or other, before they can become really deep, a definitive act of surrender, abandonment, trust or faith. To some extent it must be made in the dark. We may have plenty of grounds for trust, yet there will always be areas of mystery, of possible misunderstanding. Sooner or later we have to take that person absolutely at their word, and their word alone, when they say they love us. We have to be ready to set aside our misgivings, reservations and doubts, and choose to stand not on ourselves and what we feel, but on the word of another. By doing so, we leave ourselves and pass over to the other. We can say that we die to ourselves in order to live by the other, and the more total the commitment, the more real the death to self. To approach marriage having made most careful provision for ourselves should the other prove faithless, to have taken every precaution against such an eventuality, is to make the whole thing a farce.

It is like this between God and us. Something very similar

I make pre-nups with God

to what is demanded in human relationships is demanded here. Human beings, even the very best, are frail and untrustworthy by their sheer limitation if not by their moral weakness. God is utterly trustworthy. Nevertheless, we are not going to feel that he is. There may be much, very much indeed which, to our poor human understanding, may seem the opposite. The love-union guaranteed is not on the level which we can appreciate, not one in which we can take sensible satisfacton, and so a still more radical act of faith is demanded. We have to trust blindly that this God whom we cannot savour or appreciate *is* his own reward. We have to go further still if we would reach the fulness of faith and be concerned only that he has what he wants, that he be simply the God he is, regardless of ourselves. Because he is the God of love and his joy is our happiness, to will God to be God is my supreme happiness – but it will not be an immediate, tangible one.

The ideal love between husband and wife is God's chosen image of his relationship with us. It is a movement towards oneness or identification, an identification which paradoxically ensures the 'I' and the 'Thou'. Human love, no matter how strong and deep, must always fall short of its aim. Finite as it is, the human personality must remain for its sheer preservation ultimately 'closed'. True, it can never become itself unless it is always trying to go out from itself, to give itself, opening its portals wide;

> But there is one heart you
> shall never take him to!
>
> The hold that falls not when the town is got,
> The heart's heart, whose immurèd plot
> Hath keys yourself keep not.
> *A Fallen Yew*   F. Thompson.

There is an isolation belonging to its very being, which of itself it cannot transcend. Only in God can it be transcended and this is what God offers to man.

B

In practice, we can never separate faith and love as we can never separate knowledge and love. There can be no true knowledge that is not born of love and is part of love. We might know a lot about Jack but we don't know him. Only his intimate friend knows him. Knowledge about him can help towards love but eventually it must bend to that knowledge of him which is the fruit of love. So with God. True knowledge of God is infused, it is something we can never acquire, but if we want to love him, a way of showing love, a way of loving is to do what we can to know about him, and he has given us what we need for such knowledge. He has spoken in word and deed of what he is and this must always mean what he is to us. We are called upon to make our mind up in exactly the same way as in human affairs, but first of all we have to assure ourselves, as best we can, that it is he who is speaking through these means. Sooner or later we have to make a decision. We have to choose to believe or reject belief. The great, fundamental question put to us, in which all else is contained, is precisely 'do you believe in the Son of Man?' Ultimately it will mean a leap in the dark, for faith always demands that, otherwise it would not be faith but reason working to its conclusions logically.

To have made a decision for Jesus is not the end but the beginning. This decision has to be lived out every day. The whole of our life must be lived in its light. It will be tested, and perhaps severely. There will be times when the first decision, which then seemed definitive, is completely eclipsed by what is demanded later, and on it goes. We shall need to affirm over and over again, at ever deepening levels, our commitment to God, not because of the possibility of God failing us, for that is inconceivable, but because we shall grow in stature and will be faced with more searching, all-embracing occasions of surrender. The culmination will be when, under his influence, we have grown to our complete stature and can relate to him in that fullness of relationship for which he made us. This will mean that we have died to ourself and live in and for God.

When we are speaking of our life in God in its mortal span, although we are, theoretically, right to put the accent on love, I feel we are more helped practically to put the stress on faith and trust. We can talk eloquently about love and it can mean nothing if not accompanied by, or rather not grounded in faith – it is easy to say, 'I love you', quite a different matter to cut the ground from under our feet and trust you with our life. Whereas wherever there is faith and trust there is love, and the latter precisely in the measure of the former.

Having looked to some extent at what we might mean by believing in Jesus, now we must think about Jesus himself. Who and what is he? What is his role in our life?

2

Who is he, Lord?

We are to love God with our whole mind. The intellectual search for God, according to individual capacity, is of first importance. Yet we must always remember that the Holy Spirit alone can show us who Jesus really is, and in giving us knowledge of Jesus, show us the Father. Our human minds and the concepts they give birth to are only his lowly hand-maids. We must manage to hold these two factors together: we must do what we can to get to know our Lord, and if we do so with humble love, the Holy Spirit will light up the data from within and reveal to our hearts the inner meaning and the true face of God. On the whole, we do not advert sufficiently to this working of the Holy Spirit, we are so engrossed in and fascinated by our intellectual structures that we do not listen to him.

We erect our imposing buildings of thought, room upon room, towering majestically to the sky. We ourselves are living on the common-place ground-floor and all that soars above – lofty conceptions of the emanation of the three divine persons, dogma upon dogma of the incarnation, how the Lord is both God and man without confusion of nature and so forth – might just as well not exist for all it means to our daily life. We can come outside every now and then and take a look up and that gives us a sense of security, or we can proudly show off the edifice to another. But everything God has revealed is for living, is for use. If we seriously want God then we have to think out for ourselves what the various formulations of faith really mean to us. We must not rest content with rattling off the answer given us by others. We have to see its relevance in our life and not be content until we have done so and we are living by its truth. Hence the need for incessant pondering on the word of God. It is startling to see how little even those who have given up their lives to spirituality know of the gospels. How readily they assume something is there and something else is not because others have said so, because they have met it in books. This is no excuse. We must study the word of God ourselves, with what ability he has given us. No great gifts are needed, although in the measure of our ability and opportunity, the more use we make of modern scholarship in the understanding of the scriptures the better. However, it is ultimately faith, the earnest desire with which we approach them, that really counts. The Holy Spirit is always there enlightening our heart within the measure which we allow him. How we should devour the word of God, feed on it, take it right into ourselves, bend over it with yearning hearts, yearning to make it our life. This is to make him our life. This is no mere intellectual exercise, and the simplest can do it. It is the work of love.

Many religious people are afraid to think about the content of their faith, afraid to listen to the questions raised by modern man. Too often those who raise the questions are branded out of hand as non-believers and heretics. This attitude argues to a lack of faith, a great insecurity about faith. If faith is strong we can afford to listen, afford to think, afford to face the enormous problems which confront us and perhaps help to reach the right answers. We have absolute certainty in Jesus and what he has revealed of his Father. That is the rock on which we stand and from which nothing can shift us. From this rock we can view the troubled landscape serenely but realistically. What we must accept – and this is hard for some of us – is how little we know, or rather how much we do not know and must not pretend to know. We want a God we can hold within our minds and categories of thought. We want to understand him and be able to predict how he will act. We do not want dark areas. Whereas we must accept being led into the darkness of his mystery, a darkness which is truly luminous in the Holy Spirit. But while we cling to our formulas as though they were God himself, we shall never know that luminous darkness which is developed faith, faith which is pure gift, a share of God's own knowledge communicated directly to the human spirit.

Are not conscientious agnostics and atheists often nearer to the kingdom than its chosen children? What they are rejecting is not God but that caricature of God and of Jesus, which would be blasphemous were it not innocent, presented to the world by many christians, and not mere nominal christians but those who pride themselves on their upholding of the faith. It seems to me that this rejection honours God far more than the attitude of the smug christian who thinks he has all the answers. Our theology books speak of the *sensus fidelium*, the instinct of the people of God to discern the truth. What we may overlook is that this instinct for truth will be in exact proportion to the holiness or closeness to God of the individual members of the church. We have divine guarantee that the truth will never wholly disappear from the earth but no guarantee that it will not be distorted or defaced by our sin-blinded hearts.

If the individuals that go to make up the church, both leaders and people, are worldly, self-seeking in one way or another, narrow-minded, harsh, arrogant, lazy and unable to trust, how can the Holy Spirit make his truth known? It is only the heart that obediently listens to the word and carries it out that can be led by him into all truth, a truth which will always be the truth of Jesus. 'He shall bear witness to me'. He will tell us who Jesus really is, and all our welfare depends on that. When we know him truly, then we become witnesses in our turn and our testimony will be true, for we shall have seen and heard him at first hand. We tend to place the whole responsibility for the preservation of truth on what we call the

teaching church. Each of us must realise that we, as individuals, carry responsibility for this, a responsibility we must
carry before God for ever.

I have seen a greater grasp of the truth of Jesus in some
lay people who would not for a moment consider themselves
spiritual than among religious and those commissioned to
preach him. Because for one reason or another their intellectual grasp and verbal formulation of dogma leave much to be
desired, there can still be elements which are naive and crude.
I have noticed, however, that somehow or other the content
has filled out and overflowed the banks. We must never forget
that formulations are only formulations, only one way of trying to express a truth which infinitely transcends conceptual
knowledge, let alone formulation. Truth will always be forcing
its way through, like a child in a tight garment. So it is with
these people. At the only level that matters, that by which they
live, they know the truth. They face up to life, allow its problems and threats to get at them and do not immure themselves
behind pious platitudes. These people, whilst still reciting old
formulas, have in their own way discerned the truth hidden
within what the professional theologian is wrestling with in
words and concepts. It is not a formula, now outworn, that
has been their security. They have sought God and found him
hidden in those poor rags.

This is especially so in those matters which impinge upon
them most, death for instance. I have met a maturer view of
death here than in many religious, who tend to romanticise it.
Death is seen as it is in itself, horrible and frightening. It is
seen as the occasion for blind trust in what Jesus has promised.
'I could easily hold that death is the end and easily understand those who think so. I know it is not, because Jesus has
told us so'. Again, they have shaken off the puritanical fetters
in which they were brought up. They really understand that
God is love, is Father. They do not attribute the sorrows that
fall to them as his doing, still less his punishment. 'What have
I done that this should happen to me?' This age-long, ever-

recurring plaint which reveals, if seriously meant, a total misunderstanding of God, is never in their minds. They are not
scandalised or overthrown when their prayers 'are not heard'.
The false attitude that 'prayer will do all things; we must pray
and then this will happen or that will happen' is alien to them.

I know an old man who cherishes a great devotion to his
guardian angel. Intimacy with him has shown me quite clearly
that the guardian angel is a sort of stand-in figure with which
he can cope, for the Holy Spirit with whom he cannot cope
in the sense of think about him. And I see that through this
figure he is in continual communion with God.

Recently an elderly woman was telling me of her sorrow
at the realisation of her unkindness to her parents long ago.
They were dead and she had no means of showing them her
sorrow and love. Sorrow was with her night and day and could
easily have been nothing more than fruitless remorse, especially
as she is of a masochistic turn of mind, but faith enlightened
her. She was in a painful situation where people were unkind
to her. She could have got out of it but not without hurting
others. She realised that here was her chance to make reparation, reparation in the true sense – not mere submission to
suffering as though God or anyone else benefited by that, but
by loving those people who were unkind to her. 'I have failed
in love and this is my chance to love'. This is the sort of knowledge I mean. The Holy Spirit inspires these open, loving
hearts with the sentiments of Jesus.

I cannot understand a love that is not always wanting to
know more of the beloved so that it may love the more. 'Who
are you, Lord?' should surely be the constant urging of our
hearts. But is it so? It seems more likely that we are afraid to
get to know more, as though if we did so our building would
collapse. This is because we are putting our security not in the
unfailing God but in our meagre conceptions of him, in the
formulations, neat, satisfying, water-tight which we have con-
trived. Many of us see the church and the faith, as we call it,
like an insulated, armoured, electrified carriage in which we

can sit secure behind curtained windows as we hurtle through the dark forests. We don't have to see the frightening forms outside, don't have to see the abysses into which we might drop, don't have to see the poor beggars and forsaken ones crying in the night. We can hurtle along safely to heaven. How different from the reality! 'Do not think I have come to bring peace but a sword. I have come to cast fire on the earth.' The true experience of faith is more that of an assault on Everest with its effort, its perils, its frightening decisions. Or, in biblical imagery, a frail boat tossed like a cockle shell on the waves with not a chance of survival in itself. Only the presence of the Lord is its security, and he is asleep, seemingly inactive.

Images aside, the experience is that of the disciples, or rather of Jesus himself, when the world collapsed about him, the powers of darkness closed in and he was swallowed up. His only certainty and security lay in the love of his Father, the Father who no longer showed his face. This is what faith is about. And this is what it means to seek to know the Lord. It is, as Jesus says, when the sun is darkened, and the moon eclipsed, when the very stars are falling from heaven and our world rocking on its base – our secure, safe world – that the sign of the Son of Man is seen in glory. Then it is, if we choose, that we see him for the first time and hail him as our saviour; then we can look up in hope, heads held high, because the time of our deliverance has come.

3

The only Saviour

'There is salvation in no one else, for there is no other name under heaven given among men by which we must be saved'. (Acts 4 : 12).

This ringing proclamation of the first witness of Jesus is for all nations, all ages. It is a statement of essential christian belief. All the writers of the new testament, in their different ways, are expounding this basic truth. To those who for one reason or another are aware of their need of a saviour they are saying : 'Here he is, a man like yourself, a merciful compassionate high priest and saviour. Come to him, he will heal your ills. He will enable you to see, healing your blindness; enable you to run to God, healing your lameness; your defiling leprosy of sin will disapear at his touch. You are crushed beneath the burden of life, come to him for help and strength. You grieve and mourn, he will dry your tears. Doomed men, trapped in your world of sin and grief, he is here to set you free.'

To those for whom the world is meaningless, a jig-saw puzzle without rhyme or reason they are saying : 'It all has meaning in him, he *is* its meaning. He is heir of all things, the world was created for him so that he could be its fulfilment. The universe is upheld by him. In him all things hold together, forming one, glorious unity, utterly secure in the love of God. He is taking the world with him to his Father'.

To those who pride themselves on their religious knowledge,

sure that they hold God within their grasp, they are saying :
'You know nothing, your wisdom is folly, the fruit of pride.
You think to save yourselves and you cannot. You have only
one saviour and he is the man, Jesus, crucified as a felon on a
cross of shame. You must humbly bow before this disposition
of God, set aside your own wisdom, think different thoughts of
God learned from him in whom all wisdom dwells, if you
would be truly wise and come to God.'

Apart from Jesus we know nothing of God. This is what
these witnesses are saying. But seeing him we see the Father.

This absolute claim of Jesus' unique mediatorship is little
accepted in practice. Even in theory, when the point is pressed
home, it is rejected by some thinking christians. I had an
instance of this not long ago. I was speaking to a thoughtful
man whose life was devoted to religion. I was saying that we
have no knowledge of God apart from Jesus, that the word
'God', apart from him, is just a metaphysical concept and
almost meaningless. He denied this. What of the vast multitude
who have never known Jesus, are they debarred? There are
millions of people who know and love God yet who positively
deny this role to Jesus, he insisted.

'No one comes to the Father but by me'; the claim is absolute, categorical, but does not imply an explicit knowledge.
The same evangelist who gave us this unequivocal statement
of Jesus' mediatorship, is the one who clearly shows that Jesus
has followers among those who do not know him explicitly : 'I
have other sheep, that are not of this fold; I must bring them
also, and they will hear my voice' (Jn 10 : 16). Jesus died, he
says, 'to gather into one the children of God who are scattered
abroad' (Jn 11 : 52) in every age, in every race. In my endeavour to express what believing in Jesus means, I hope it
will become clear that there are many 'not of this fold' who
are listening to his voice though they know it not, who despite
this, believe in him. They cannot name him, they may even
deny that the Lord of their hearts is Jesus, and this because
they have only met his image and his teaching in the garbled

version we have given them. The Lamb was slain from the foundation of the world and his redeemed are in every age, even before his coming in historical time. They are scattered now, unknown to themselves and to any but God.

My friend went on to say that he knew God before he knew Jesus. For him it was first God, then Jesus. The crucial word is, of course, 'God'. We have St Paul telling the Romans of the God they can know from the observation of visible things. But he is essentially the 'unknown God' until he is revealed in Jesus. Beyond the fact that he is maker of heaven and earth we know nothing about him, nothing of the way he regards us, but in Jesus the loving-kindness of our God has appeared, he is our friend, our Father.

This religious attitude taken by my friend and freely expressed is, I think, extremely common even though those holding it might be aghast at his frank avowal. Basic to this attitude is lack of faith. We don't need faith to acknowledge 'God'. He is the product of our own selves, a god fashioned in our own image and likeness. How could he not be? Left to ourselves we can only have finite ideas and images and our god is fashioned of these. We are dealing with a god we can compass with our minds and deal with him there. Even though we delight in stretching our minds and saying 'beyond, beyond, beyond that . . .' it still remains a natural exercise within natural bounds and can never attain the infinite God. He has chosen to reveal himself in Jesus and only when we are prepared to abdicate from our own ground and go over to Jesus by a leap in the dark can we know God, and to know God means to attain him or be united with him. As I said earlier, knowledge in the spiritual sense is inseparable from love and union. The measure of our knowledge is the measure of our union; the measure of our union is in proportion to our knowledge, not a conceptual knowledge but the knowledge infused by God which is faith.

The god we mould for ourselves usually has two faces; one that beams upon us and flatters our ego, intercourse with whom 'glorifies' us; one that sternly appraises us, demanding a standard we cannot possibly reach. At all costs we must be placating this god, making ourselves safe against him. We must make sure there is not a thing in which he can catch us out; make sure we give him his quota of worship and torment ourselves if we cannot manage it. He must not be allowed to get at us. Don't we long to be told just what to do? 'Tell me what to do at prayer and I will do it'. What we are saying is that we will do anything, anything at all but trust ourselves to God. This is understandable enough when we do not know God, the Father of Jesus. Perversely, we do not want to know him, the source of all our happiness, and the reason is because it will demand a relinquishing of our most cherished possession, the control we have over ourselves, the power which we think we have to seek and find God on our own terms, our own spiritual achievement.

For many, I venture to say for most, there would be no significant difference in their religious attitude if the incarnation had not taken place, if there were no Jesus. Moreover I have in mind people who pray to Jesus, who pray in his name, who frequent the sacraments. What has happened is that we have merely transferred our notion of God to Jesus. Instead of looking at Jesus to learn what God is like and how we go to him, we project on to Jesus our ideas of God and so lose sight of him and his essential message. We still think, if not perhaps explicitly because we have been taught differently, that we must do all this ourselves. We have formed our own ideas of what God wants us to be like and are earnestly striving for self-perfection. We are really reversing roles. We are trying to be God in making him better off through what we give him. We want to make him a present of our own perfect selves. This has nothing to do with holiness. Only Jesus is holy, the only one pleasing to his Father. Only by allowing him to communicate his holiness to us can we be pleasing to God.

To be in the Father's heart – this is what it is all about. This is what salvation means. Jesus and Jesus alone is the Father's

beloved. He has a unique relationship with his Father, which
is his innermost meaning. John shows us this in page upon
page of his gospel. Jesus is the only one who has seen and
knows God; everything the Father has is his; all the Father's
secrets are communicated to him. What the Father does, he
does. His eyes are fixed upon the Father and he imitates him
in all things. He is the perfect revelation of the Father in
human terms. When we say Jesus is God we mean this unique
relationship with his Father. We mean that he is not merely
man, that it is not possible to push his relationship with his
Father too far. The relationship of love which he has with his
Father is to be shared with us. There is no other relationship
we can claim. It is only by entering into Jesus' relationship
with God that we can be in his heart. The only begotten is in
the bosom of the Father, nearest to his heart; the beloved
disciple is on the bosom of Jesus and drawn by him into the
Father's heart, with him, where he is.

The synoptists have their own particular way of expressing
their understanding of this innermost reality of Jesus. It is
the story of the transfiguration. Those who lived with Jesus
in his public life, heard him, saw him, touched him with their
hands, had no doubt at all that he was a man. They saw him
eat and sleep, weep and smile; they heard him groan in
anguish and fall flat on his face in tormented entreaty. They
saw him die on the cross. A man like them and yet there was
a difference. Perhaps they discussed it among themselves.
What was it that set him apart? They sensed another dimension to him. When the Son of Man had risen from the dead,
they saw it. It was his closeness to God whom he called his
Father. A unique closeness far beyond anything they could
fathom. This was his heartbeat, what made him tick. What
they had dimly surmised all along was now clear. To express
it they drew on the Old Testament imagery of God's closeness.
Jesus goes up a mountain, the place of revelation where
heaven stoops down to earth. Two great figures, Moses and
Elijah, to whom a theophany was granted in their life time,

are seen conversing with Jesus. Jesus is aglow, face and raiment, with the nearness of God; the sacred cloud, symbol of God's very presence, overshadows and envelops him and a voice from the cloud proclaims him as his beloved son, his delight, the one to whom men must listen.

Dimly aware of Jesus' intimacy with God, they realised too that it was in a context of suffering. Throughout his life Jesus' love for his Father and for us was sacrificial. All John's great signs, in which the glory of God in Jesus flashed forth, are set against the background of the paschal sacrifice and the cross of the Lord. The synoptists reveal this understanding too in the story of the transfiguration. In the encounter of love and acceptance Jesus is conversing with Moses and Elijah, and the theme is his death; all Jerusalem is to see the ecstasy of love with which he died. In their daily converse with him his disciples did not wish to hear of it; Peter tried to turn him aside from this course; Jesus insisted. Now the Father bids them listen to Jesus. 'For you too there must be a death, a going forth from yourselves, an ecstasy of love, so that you might come to me with the Beloved, to live no longer with your own impoverished, corruptible life, but with my own radiant, eternal life. You were made for this. All that is made was made for this; Come, receive your kingdom!'

Mortal man may encounter God in such a way as to be transformed by him. God himself can strike a man as lightning strikes, not for his destruction but to create him anew. This work of transformation is effected only in and through Jesus. It is a share of Jesus' own union with his Father. We have to come to him, to believe in him, receive him and he, in his turn, takes over and bears us to the Father. For us, as for him, there is only one path, the way of the cross. In essence, this means consenting to be taken beyond our limitations, to die that we might live. We cannot have our own life and God's life at the same time. The ultimate relinquishing of our own life takes place at death, but death will only be death in Jesus in the measure that we have already yielded up our life to him, handed it over, allowed him to bring us to a new birth, clothed head to foot in Christ. Faith is that movement whereby we accept God's nearness, and his nearness must always mean the death of the ego.

There is nothing in scripture to tell us that, in this life, transformation into Jesus will be experienced as a state of bliss. Quite the contrary. Jesus died in an ecstasy of love but what was his experience? Paul reveals to us how much those for whom Christ has become their life must bear for his sake.

4

The word of the cross

To maintain, as a christian must, that Jesus is our only way to
the Father and that we go to the Father only by entering into
his death, will have the most far-reaching implications in our
life. All christians give intellectual assent to this truth and in
certain ways attempt to apply it. Every instructor in the christian way will show us how we must accept the trials of life,
overcome our bad tendencies and practise self-denial. This is
to share in the death of Jesus. But it may not take place.
Every thing we do, however good in itself, instead of being a
share in Jesus' death may become a means of fostering our
own life at the expense of his. We share in his death when
we consent to abdicate before him, when we allow him to
work in us and do the work for us. Instead we usually prefer
to hold on to the reins ourselves. We see ourselves as the agents
of our own sanctification, God being there simply to help us.
Whatever our intellectual assent to christianity, until we have
learned to trust God with our spiritual development we are
still in the sphere of natural religion, trying to reach him by
our own effort.

A great deal of Jesus' moral teaching was already man's
heritage, bequeathed by noble, pure-hearted men throughout
the ages. Jesus reaffirmed and took up into himself everything
authentically human. Everything that is truly human is pointing towards God and moving towards him. Jesus takes it upon
his back and carries it to the destiny it could never otherwise
reach. Some great natural religions share much of the ethics

of the gospel. What is unique to christianity and at its heart is the recognition that it is God who sanctifies us, that we ourselves cannot add one cubit to our spiritual stature. Of ourselves we can do nothing at all. All that we do, our very uttermost, which nevertheless we have to do, is merely a preparation for that direct intervention of God which alone can bring us to himself. Natural religion is essentially man's effort to reach God. Christianity demands a death; it brings it about. In some mysterious way man must die to himself in order to receive new life as a pure gift from God. There must be a new creation, a rebirth. Man cannot evolve into holiness through personal effort and discipline no matter how spiritual and sublime. There is an absolute gulf between the life of God and the life of man to cross which man must die. Christianity is mystical to the core, understanding by 'mystical' the direct intervention and operation of God in a human being, God touching man in a way quite distinct from that ordinary presence and assistance to men without which they could not exist, let alone act and grow.

Because the death spoken of here has been grossly misunderstood in a way that can never be justified by the scriptures, even if an isolated text or two seemed to support it, christianity is despised and feared as inhuman, negative, a kill-joy religion that never allows man freedom to live in this world. Misunderstanding the nature of his death, men have tried to induce it by inflicting every manner of deprivation on themselves, withdrawing as much as possible from all that goes to make up the fabric of human life, accepting the barest minimum as essential to survival. Man must not be allowed to develop his natural potentialities, these could lead to his ruin; he must not be allowed to enjoy pleasure. He must die to everything in this world and only then will he live to God.

The truth is that a man could live the most austere life, dying in all but physical death, yet still be very much alive, perhaps more than ever so, with his own life. Austerities are impressive, as Paul says to the Colossians (Col 2 : 23) seeming to promote rigour of devotion and self-abasement, but they are powerless to overcome our basic self-indulgence; in fact they increase it. Any spirituality which seeks to induce what is in reality a mystical death by a false denial of this world, meaning a denial of our human condition, is opposed to christianity. Mystical death comes from divine contact, direct confrontation with Jesus; it is an entry into his death. 'No one can come to me unless it is granted him by the Father' (Jn 6 : 65). All we can do is prepare for this grace, and the preparation demands a love-directed asceticism which is far removed from the activity just described.

Wrong ideas of this death have led to a distortion of christianity which has rightly won contempt, but we have to note that a true understanding of it, or rather that measure of understanding which we can gain before we ourselves enter into it and know its beatitude, must cause revulsion. It is not only a distortion of christianity that is rejected but the reality, and precisely because at its core lies this death which cuts clean across man's pride, pierces him at his most sensitive spot, his ego. It calls for a profound humility, and humility is not an attitude native to man; it is not on the list of virtues which make us human. It enters the scene only with revelation, only with Jesus who is humility personified, the love which empties self in order to give itself to the beloved. And Jesus is the revelation of the Father. Humility has everything to do with love.

For John the whole of Jesus' mortal life, and the revelation of God which that mortal life embodied was sealed with his death. The high point of revelation, when the glory of God's love shone out and his inmost heart was laid bare, was when Jesus died on the cross. We take this for granted, we say it lightly, but do we grasp an atom of its significance for us? As Paul says, this is the great scandal, and Peter too : ' "Behold I am laying in Zion a stone, a cornerstone chosen and precious, and he who believes in him will not be put to shame". To you therefore who believe, he is precious, but for those who do not believe, "The very stone which the builders rejected has become the head of the corner", and "A stone that will make men stumble, a rock that will make them fall" ' (1 Pet : 6–8).

We must not think that just because we are professing christians, because we pray, frequent the sacraments and try to live good lives that we have thereby, in John's sense, 'come' to Jesus, 'believe' in him. A careful reading of John might shake our happy certainty and for our gain. 'Now when he was in Jerusalem for the Passover feast, many believed in his name when they saw the signs which he did; but Jesus did not trust himself to them' (Jn 2 : 23–24). Are we sure that Jesus has trusted himself to us, he who knows men so well?

Again, 'Though he had done so many signs before them, yet they did not believe in him; it was that the word spoken by the prophet Isaiah might be fulfilled : "Lord, who has believed our report, and to whom has the arm of the Lord been revealed?" ' (Jn 12 : 37–38). Significantly, the text cited here comes from Isaiah's lament at the people's rejection of the Lord's suffering servant : 'He had no form or comeliness that we should look at him, and no beauty that we should desire him. He was despised and rejected by men; a man of sorrows, and acquainted with grief; as one from whom men hide their faces he was despised, and we esteemed him not' (Is 53 : 2–3). This is the 'report' of John, and this is what we reject.

God does not answer man's expectations, the expectation of pride, of flesh and blood, not of the Spirit of God who wills all that is best for man. God does not do what man expects him to do, does not approach him in the form he wants, which at the deepest level means that God, far from boosting man and making him feel grand, does exactly the opposite. The effect of God drawing close to us always means that what Isaiah said of the suffering servant becomes true for us. In a very deep way we have to sacrifice that which seems to make us man, what we think of as a beautiful spirituality; we have to be changed in a way that *seems* to make us less, not more

human. There is nothing here naturally attractive to man;
rather, his instinct must be to turn away in revulsion. This,
in practice, in hard reality, is what it means to embrace Jesus
crucified, and embracing him, embrace he who sent him and
whose revelation he is.

Paul, like John, was sadly aware that the magnificent gift
of God offered to man met with little response. He had bitter
proof in his own converts. He had to berate them for their
gross immorality, they who by their baptism, the rite of incor-
poration into Jesus, should be temples of the Holy Spirit. Children of God in name, look how they behave! They are still
'in the flesh'. Yet it was not only immoral behaviour that
worried Paul. He saw there was a still greater obstacle, greater
because more subtle and less obvious, to the grace of Jesus, to
the word of the cross. Though christian in name, some of his
converts were still staking everything on their observance of
the law, still tying themselves up with exterior practices of
devotion, still relying on their own efforts to reach God. Once
this had been true of him; he had seen himself as the agent of
his own righteousness, but so radical was his conversion that
there was no question of return. I feel he was shocked to find
it was not so with others.

His own conversion was complete according to the grace of
the moment. 'Not that I have already obtained or am already
perfect; but I press on to make it my own, because Christ
Jesus has made me his own' (Phil 3 : 12). To speak of Paul's
conversion as the conversion of a sinner in the sense we usually
mean is to miss the point entirely. Paul was not a sinner in
this sense, he was a deeply religious man, blameless in the
keeping of the law. Nor is there question of mere outward
observance, he strove for purity of heart. In Romans he tells
us of his struggle to control his bad instincts and, as Dodd
observes, the one he actually mentions is a wholly interior one,
covetousness. Paul was not a hypocrite, ostentatious, intent
only on outward show as the synoptists show us the Pharisees
to be; he acted from a sincere heart.

The sudden encounter with the Lord upset his whole range of values and turned his spiritual world upside down. What hitherto he had regarded as a revolting scandal, utterly loathsome even to consider, namely that a man, crucified as felon, condemned by the law, was God's messiah became now his only boast. It is hard for us to grasp the scandal this was for him, we who revere the cross, hailing it as the blessed sign of our redemption. For Paul it was anathema, the clean opposite of every idea he had of the God of his fathers and of the messiah he could expect. For him the cross was the very symbol of shame and godlessness. His encounter with the Lord changed all this in a moment. The cross became the centre of his existence, the only content of his preaching. His physical blindness was a symbol of the destruction of the worldly wisdom which had blinded him to the truth and was now overcome by the folly of the cross. Paul, unlike the vast majority to whom the same grace was offered, accepted it with all his heart, and God was able to give him the fullness of what he offered. He bowed his whole being before the crucified; everything that had been built up in him, all that of which he had been proud – his Hebrew ancestry, his pharisaical training, the righteousness he had acquired through self-discipline and effort, all was cast aside; it gave him not a scrap of claim to God's love; he saw clearly that no human creature could earn God's love, could wave his achievements before God to win his approval. God gave his love freely in and through the man Jesus. Paul was happy to have no righteousness of his own but only that which comes through Jesus. This is what Paul meant by dying with Jesus; he died to himself and all that had gone before. He accepted being created anew in Christ Jesus. His baptism was the acting out in rite of what had already happened. He had gone down into the waters of death with Jesus and risen with his life. The inmost reality really matched the sign.

It is simply not true of the majority of us, and now I am meaning good, spiritual people, that we believe in Jesus and make him the centre of our lives. We are more where Paul was before the Lord struck him down. When he tries to get at us in the same way, when he cuts into our lives, then we leave him and walk no more with him, even though on a superficial level we still remain in his company.

To become a true disciple of Jesus means accepting a spirituality of the cross and renouncing a spirituality of glory. The first is of God, the second of man, of 'flesh and blood'. As I have pointed out earlier, there is no question of it being merely a matter of hard or easy, the spirituality of the cross being full of hard things, and the spirituality of glory full of nice things. The contrary may be true. It has nothing to do with hard or easy in that sense. It has everything to do with seeking God and not self. The spirituality of glory seeks itself under cover of God. It seeks a boost, wants proofs, testimonies from within or without, excitement, feelings, miracles, success – all that flatters human pride. The spirituality of the cross seeks God and accepts having none of those things; if they are there it refuses to overvalue them or attach significance to them. It knows that God cannot be grasped with our ordinary powers and accepts deprivation on that level.

One of the disturbing features of the modern interest in prayer which I referred to in the Introduction is this concern with feelings and 'things happening'. I do not want to be damping in my criticism, but when it is said that people today, particularly the young, are fascinated by prayer – offer a talk on prayer and you get a full house – it sets me thinking. It seems to be the in-thing and every effort is made to make it interesting. Prayer can never be separated from life. Does this prayer involve their whole life? Are they struggling to overcome their bad tendencies, their selfishness, and are they trying to fulfil the law of God? If they are, fine. Will they maintain interest in prayer only while prayer is interesting? Unless those engaged in helping people bear all this in mind, little will be achieved. On the contrary, people will be kept back. When God wants to lead them further they will be encouraged, not to respond but to turn away and try to recover the natural enthusiasm, feelings, and excitement in prayer which they have lost. It is one thing to have these things – a carrot to the unwilling donkey – but quite another to lay stress on them and consider them important.

The doctrine here upheld is out of date, or at least dated. It belongs to a particular era in the development of the church and is an off-shoot of platonism and its semi-christian off-spring. John of the Cross is its chief exponent. He is the doctor of mystical darkness. Granted this is an authentic way, it is not the only way. There is equally a doctrine of mystical light and this is the atmosphere of modern spirituality.

What is meant here by 'mystical light' is simply emotional experience, feelings of God's presence and the like. We must firmly maintain that these experiences, of themselves, have no spiritual significance. To seek and highly value 'experience', no matter how spiritual, is to choose a created reality instead of God, and ultimately self instead of God. Our psychic powers may echo and tremble at the touch of God but we have no proof that what happens on the psychic level emanates from the touch of God in our depths. It could just as easily come from other sources. Surely our common-sense and practical experience tell us that, but we don't see what we don't want to see.

Because of the rapid development of technology we live in an atmosphere of uncertainty and threat. Earlier generations had certainties, we have none. It isn't only that we can blow ourselves up at any time but on the religious plane itself, is anything held to be certain? What can we be sure of? It is very hard for sensitive people to live with this acute insecurity and there is a longing to grasp at something tangibly certain; they want proof that God is *there*, in his world, with them. They want to feel that they really matter to God. Testimonies, marvellous answers to prayer, miracles, intense feelings of God's presence, the support of others in these things, all help to provide this sustaining sense of the reality of God.

This is most understandable and one can sympathise. Still, it is to shirk the cross. Christianity can never be easy. We might think that earlier generations had greater helps to faith than we have today. It could be truer to say they had more substitutes for faith : so many things in our universe remained a mystery and could easily be attributed to God; it was relatively easy to 'believe' in him. With terrible ruthlessness these substitutes have been snatched away. Should we lament? We should recognise rather that now, as never before, we are offered the venture of faith. We are being forced to naked faith, to that alone, and this is a privilege. We are not left alone, far from it. The mighty power of God is at hand to operate in our poverty and weakness. But what are we doing but putting in substitutes for those that have been taken away, making ourselves powerful and strong? Faith certainly needs supports; it needs no substitutes.

5

The narrow gate

From the foregoing it should be clear that the division of our spiritual journey into three stages is no fanciful fabrication but arises from the very nature of things, God being what he is and we being what we are. They are distinct stages of nearness to God. To begin with we have not yet 'come' to Jesus even though we are in his company and want to learn from him. Like Nicodemus we draw near to Jesus in our night of ignorance. Not that Nicodemus thought himself ignorant! We make an act of faith, an all-important, primal one, 'We know that you are a teacher come from God'. Jesus, in mysterious language, tries to make Nicodemus understand what must happen if he is to go further, if he is to enter the kingdom, that sphere where God, not man, is in supreme control, where God gives and man receives. The master of Israel must, like Paul, lay aside his own ideas and consent to become a little child. Nicodemus considers himself a virtuous, wise man and Jesus is telling him this wisdom and virtue will get him nowhere. He is still trapped in the sphere of the flesh, and flesh can never attain God. In the word 'flesh' there is no suggestion of body as distinct from spirit. What is meant is man as he is in himself, left to his own resources, or rather choosing to depend on his own resources, for God is always offering to take over. Jesus impresses on this great man his complete helplessness in the things of God. You cannot control the wind nor predict its movements, neither are you in control of the Spirit; you have to surrender to his control. Nico-

demus has to die to his own life and be born again, otherwise
he can never enter the kingdom.

For one who accepts this way of surrender, there follows a
long and arduous discipleship. Perfect transformation into
Jesus does not take place all at once. Man must co-operate
with the action of the Holy Spirit who is now able to operate
freely from within, where before he could only direct the mind
and heart from outside. Now the heart has opened to receive
him. This is the second stage, true discipleship. This long
discipleship will most surely lead to the last stage, transforming union, which is what christianity is all about.

The world in principle is reconciled with God through the
death and resurrection of Jesus; the Holy Spirit has been sent
among us for the remission of sin. The gate stands open before
us and no power can swing it shut. But each of us has to
choose to walk through that gate. 'Enter by the narrow gate
.... the gate is narrow and the way is hard, that leads to life,
and those who find it are few' (Mt 7 : 13–14). If they are few
it is not because what is asked is beyond our strength or ability
but because the gate is narrow. To pass through it one must
be small and unencumbered. Much must be left behind and
this 'much' really means no more than our self-importance.
Like Nicodemus, we have to become children to go through
the gate. Luke adds that we must 'strive' to enter through the
narrow gate. We have to pass from this world of sin (where
'sin' does not mean moral defection; the reverse of sin is not
moral rectitude but faith in Jesus) to God's world. It does not
happen all at once. Baptism does not achieve the passage for
us, rather it reveals and initiates what, with our whole freedom
engaged, we must labour to receive from God. It must be very
rare for the reality of baptism to fit the sign. For most of us it
is a continuing thing. We must go on trying to implement our
baptism, bring it to completion in our lives. We must labour to
have faith in Jesus and abandon ourselves to him. This is not
a matter of sentiment but of life-long effort. As John puts it,
it was to those who could stand by Jesus when humanly speak-

ing all was lost, when God had disappeared and godlessness prevailed, that Jesus bowed his head in death and gave the Spirit.

Continually we must hold two strands in our hands and not let go of one or other if we would get across what a life of deep faith entails. First, everything is gift and God must do all. Man can do nothing to bring himself to God. Secondly, man must not sit with his hands in his lap. He must act. He must do all he possibly can to grow and to respond to God and without this preparation God cannot work in man as he wishes. We have to learn from Jesus what God's will is and try to fulfil it. God isn't standing by saying: 'Now let me see you trying. When I see you have really tried, I will step in and help'. No, this delay of God is in the nature of things. God is offering himself to me here and now but I cannot receive him. I must have reached a certain level of development before I can begin to do so. New wine cannot be poured into old skins otherwise the skins are spoiled and the wine runs away. God can only come in with his mystical 'over-and-above' help when man has reached his limits and can go no further.

We live in a cave. The cave is so vast and we are so small that we cannot perceive it is a cave until we have grown in stature. It seems a limitless world, a most beautiful city full of good things, everything we need for our stimulation and growth. Here, it seems, is love and knowledge of God, here is wisdom, here true worship. The ensign of Jesus flies over its citadels. Christians recognise the ensign, they know the name of their king and wish to serve him. There is no need to question the *raison d'être* of this city; it seems to exist in its own right and needs no explanation apart from itself. How can there be anywhere else except heaven when this mortal life is over?

In reality, the cave does not exist for itself but exclusively for another world, the kingdom of God where even in this life he truly reigns over human hearts. Were it not so, were there no way out of it, it would be nothing but a great trap, a hideous mockery; we would be trapped for ever in our own limitations, our innate yearning for God thwarted for ever. Redemption means there is a way out. Jesus has made the way. He is the gate through which we pass, the way on which we walk and the goal of our journey. Everything God has provided for us in the cave-city is for one purpose only, to fit us for passing through that gate, out of the natural mode of existence which is 'death', into the life of God.

Although it does not seem like it, when we are in the cave we are like Lazarus in his tomb. Jesus calls to us to come out. To be brought to life from this 'dead' death is to begin to die mystically with Jesus so as to rise with his life. 'If you had been here my brother would not have died'. Where Jesus is, there is true life, but to receive it we must receive Jesus when he comes to us, however he comes. We must heed his summons to come out to him.

We prefer to be in our cave. We are secure and happy there so long as we do not know it is a cave. We do not want to see the gate and what lies beyond. Compared with the rich life of the city-cave, what lies outside, through the gate, seems bleak and featureless . . . it looks like death. Yet unless we pass through that gate we can never realise our destiny, never achieve our goal. If we do not pass through it in our mortal life we pass through it in physical death, for there is no other way to God. The initiative, the call is his, we cannot anticipate or fake it. We cannot even know of it except in a theoretical way, which means nothing until it comes. We have to do all we can to prepare for the summons and welcome it when it comes.

How does it come? Our awareness of it will be an awareness that we are, in fact, in a cave; that what we had thought of as a spiritual world has disintegrated. We see that we are trapped, confined and without hope of betterment unless someone intervenes. This is when we really appreciate that we need a saviour. It cannot happen until he have exhausted the possibilities of the cave, until we have used to the full what is offered us there. That is the exercising ground, so to speak, for the journey out. But when we have exhausted its possibilities, we know it and realise there is no way forward for us. We have reached a dead end. In effect it will mean that we see clearly that we don't love God, that we really know nothing about him; we are not spiritual or good. We thought we were doing well in the spiritual way and we see that we are not. We have got nowhere and what is more, we see that we are helpless. This always presumes a very generous effort to do everything we think God wants of us. There are many, many people in this cave who do not try or try very little and there is no likelihood of them coming to the gate. They are not sufficiently in earnest.

All along God has been helping us forward and always his grace results not in our feeling full of light and understanding, not in high feelings of devotion, but in becoming aware how poor and shoddy we are; how everything we do is riddled with selfishness. This is not an easy situation to accept – it is the last thing we want. We can bear all sorts of hardships and difficulties provided we have a spiritual self-assurance, but when that is taken away the savour of life has gone. Hitherto we have thought this self-assurance to be confidence in God; we have not realised that it is really confidence in what we have built up in ourselves by dint of hard labour. Now it is gone. Can we begin to trust in Jesus alone? There is nothing in ourselves to give us assurance. Can we rely only on his goodness? To make a definitive stand or decision here, to carry out the resolution, refusing to look back to what has gone, refusing to try to regain what we seem to have lost, is to pass through the gate and enter a wholly new dimension of human existence. It is to have 'come' to Jesus, to 'believe' in him; now he is free, in increasing measure, to communicate to us his own life, and gradually, if we are faithful, bring us to perfect union with himself and his Father.

I must stress again that all this presupposes generosity. Like the apostles, we must have laboured all night and taken nothing before Jesus can fill our nets. The labour is essential. Most of us are not generous enough. The road to life is hard but it is not tortuous or complicated; what is more, it does not cut strange ways for itself. Just because it is God's road it is on this earth, running through our days and years, running through the familiar scenery of our everyday life. To opt out of our ordinary human life is to get off the road.

I found a moving illustration of what it means to live wholeheartedly, to use to the utmost what life in the cave offers, in the book *Mister God this is Anna*. As portrayed for us, the child Anna searched for God with rare intensity. She sought for him everywhere and in everything, greedy for anything which would bring her greater understanding. Everything for her was the ore from which she could extract gold. More important still, she was prepared to accept the consequences of greater understanding. The cost often racked her with anguish. One day she attended a funeral. She had listened attentively to the paltry sermon and to a conversation among her companions on the nature of death and life afterwards, a conversation pitifully crude in its ignorance. That night Fynn was awakened by a cry of despair from Anna. Her eyes were wild, tears streamed down her cheeks and her hands were pressed against her mouth as if to stop herself screaming. He knew he was powerless to enter her solitude or comfort her in any way. She was up against naked, bruising, frightening reality. At last she spoke, not to him but to God: 'Please, please, Mister God, teach me to ask real questions. Oh please, Mister God, help me to ask real questions'.

Later on, when Fynn questioned her as to why she has asked God about real questions, she replied that it was sad, just sad that people only ask little questions of God and so they only get little answers. And to Fynn's, 'I expect we're all in some sort of prison', she replied vehemently, 'No, Mister God wouldn't do that . . . Let Mister God be. He lets us be'.

To ask God big questions means getting big answers and most of us don't want big answers so we don't ask big questions. We do not risk anything. Yet we christians are the ones who, because of Jesus, should be able to ask the biggest questions of all, fearlessly facing reality, exposing ourselves to it because this is to expose ourselves to God himself. This child did not know Jesus. She was searching in the cave and died before her emergence. Surely in death she met him and he took her to his Father.

One of the drawbacks of using literature, of seeking examples in the lives of others, is that usually the 'others', those who have written or been written about, are specially gifted on the natural level. We can easily confuse their natural gifts with their spiritual growth and the direction they give us. This child for instance. I am sure most of us could truthfully say that we have not got that sort of natural intensity. But the conclusion cannot be drawn 'therefore I simply cannot do what she did'. In a sense this is true but in another it is not. What she did was to do what she could do and go to her limits. That is what each of us can and must do and we have no excuse for not doing so. The dull, ungifted person has just the same chance of holiness as the most intelligent, intense and dynamic.

6

The pain of being human

As disciples of Jesus our heart's desire must be to 'be filled with the knowledge of his will in all spiritual wisdom and understanding, to lead a life worthy of the Lord, fully pleasing to him, bearing fruit in every good work and increasing in the knowledge of God' (Col 1 : 9–10). If we were to consult some older manuals dealing with the ascetical life, that is, how we must work in order to overcome our bad habits and acquire virtue, we would probably be given a list of virtues, shown how our Lord himself practised them in his mortal life, and counsel on how we must imitate him. Likewise we would be given systems of prayer, and rules for organising our life and governing our conduct. A programme would be set before us which we could follow quite meticulously, ticking off one point after another. The great defect of such an approach is that it concentrates on self-perfection. All the attention is on self. We glance at our Lord and imitate him only in order to perfect our behaviour and shine before him. It is possible to build a splendid structure of spirituality that has nothing to do with God and his life in us and the approach I have mentioned easily fosters this.

This is not the way to imitate Jesus. A well-worn cliché in pious circles runs : 'we must not excuse ourselves when blamed because Jesus was silent before his judges when accused'. Is this the significance of our Lord's silence in court ? Paul did not think so; he had plenty to say for himself and in no measured terms and he did not hesitate to tell his converts to

D

imitate him as he imitated Christ. Jesus' individual acts cannot be taken one by one and copied. We must get to know the inner attitudes from which all his actions sprang and make these our own. We are not Jews of ancient Palestine. We have to live according to the mind of Jesus in our own particular situation.

When we look at Paul's list of virtues which the christian must work for we find they are directed away from the self to others, to life, to reality outside ourselves. There is no question of watching every word, concentrating on details of behaviour; no fear of self-conceit. There is really only one virtue and that is love, a great, caring love for others that is patient, kind, compassionate, gentle, humble, long-suffering, tenderly considerate for the weak, always ready to put others before self. It is a love that is steadfast and enduring. Perhaps most significantly a love that 'bears all things, believes all things, hopes all things, endures all things' (1 Cor 13 : 7). A love that says 'yes' to human life in its bruising and wounding; that does not escape into a hard shell but remains quivering and exposed, never embittered, always seeing beyond appearances to the God who never fails and who holds his world and all that is in it in his love.

Though he had never seen Jesus in the flesh, Paul had, unlike any other except perhaps the evangelist John, a surpassing knowledge of him, and when he is telling his converts how they should live as the 'holy and beloved' of God, he has the figure of Jesus before the eyes of his heart. This is how Jesus lived and our lives in this world must be like his.

Jesus' fundamental earthly task, in which he expressed his love for his Father, was simply to be man, to accept our human lot to the full. The epistle to the Hebrews speaks of Jesus learning obedience, Son of God though he was. He had to learn, through sheer experience, how hard it is to be a man and to have to die. Through total acceptance of this human destiny Jesus was made perfect. The cost was bitter, ending in a cruel, humiliating death, but through it he is able to bring us all along with him to our fulfilment, provided we accept it as he did. For us, too, our fundamental obedience to God is to accept being human. There is only one path to glory and that is the way Christ took, accepting the pain of being human.

But we may say, we have no choice, we cannot help but be human. In a minimal, unimportant sense this is true. However, it is one thing to be just a member of the human species and another to become fully human, growing into a true man or a true woman. We can refuse to live in the truth of our condition and thus never reach fulfilment as a human person.

To be human means that we are a dependent being by very essence. Not only are we absolutely dependent on other persons and things for our bodily survival but we have to look beyond ourselves for our meaning. We have no fulfilment within ourselves and, what is more, we know that we are answerable not merely to ourselves but to another outside ourselves. In countless ways we are at the mercy of forces beyond our control. Our existence is given without our previous consent; our heredity and all that goes with it of temperament, mental outlook, opportunities and so forth are none of our choosing. We are conditioned from the start and can be burdened with immense handicaps and suffering. Even in those areas where theoretically we are free to choose, how many impediments come between, through tricks of fortune or the actions of others. We are frighteningly, pitifully dependent.

Nevertheless, we are answerable. We are free. In all this unfreedom and conditioning we are responsible for what we do. No one can remove this responsibility from us. We are answerable not for our temperament, not for the shape of our body, not for our natural capacity, but for what we do with these things. Our task is fundamentally the same as Jesus'. We have to live out our own individual life with its own particular amalgam, in love of God and our neighbour, bearing all things, believing all things, hoping all things, enduring all things. With all our heart we have to embrace this painful condition of dependency even when it presses most sorely, never trying to pretend that it is other than it is, never railing against it but accepting it in humble, trustful obedience to the Father, and through this loving obedience filtering out all that is evil, transforming it into gold.

Our pride urges us to escape as much as we can from whatever forces upon us our fundamental state of dependency and helplessness; love of Jesus will make us understand and embrace it, and in it find freedom. To the eye of faith it is the sacrament of our blessed dependence on God who alone is our meaning and fulfilment. The observable, experiential poverty and dependence of man is the outward sign of his profound relation to God. Man is an emptiness only God can fill. All through his life Jesus accepted being this emptiness, an existence meaningless save in its relation to God. He lived only from and for his Father and saw himself only in this relationship. The Father's will was the motive force of his life. He had nothing of his own, everything was received. He is *the* man and what is true of him must become true of us. Holiness means that a human being has so affirmed, stood by, embraced his essential meaning of being a capacity for God, an emptiness for him to fill, that God can indeed fill him with the fullness of himself.

To follow Jesus, to have his mind, means entering into his death, that is accepting the essential poverty of our human existence. This was his joy, but at a cost. 'Loud cries and tears' and urgent supplication to be saved from the full rigour of this dispossession of self accompanied his perfect obedience. We need not be ashamed of our shrinking and disgust.

At every turn of life we come up against our limitations. We are ignorant and make mistakes even with the best will in the world, and the consequences of these innocent mistakes can be terrible and far-reaching, affecting not only ourselves but many others. Though Jesus never committed sin, he too was subject to ignorance and consequent fallibility. Have we any reason for thinking that he never knew the agony of indecision : which is the best course? Or the agony of doubt : have

I made a mistake, is the failure due to an error of judgment? Have I failed because I was too harsh and outspoken with the Pharisees? Like us he had nothing to lean on but the love and fidelity of his Father, who knows the stuff of which we are made. To have to live with the consequences of our own mistakes, let alone our sin, is a hard thing indeed, but we must live with them not in bitterness but in humble trust and love.

There are some in the world, a privileged few, who are able to choose their work, their environment, and to a great extent shield themselves from many of the hardships others, lacking these advantages, must suffer. The vast majority of men are not in a position to choose their work or their living conditions. They must take on any job that will earn their daily bread. They are not in a position to win privileges or protect themselves from hardship. They suffer from natural forces, they suffer from the injustices of others. Jesus' destiny was to identify himself with these unprivileged ones, to become one of the common people. The very death he died shows us that. Had he been privileged he might have saved himself; influential friends, his own status and name would have been his allies. As it was, a common man of the people, he was helpless.

There is another form of human helplessness and littleness which he did not choose to share, presumably because he saw it as unimportant in itself. What I mean is lack of personal stature. There are many 'small' people to whom no one ever listens simply because they lack presence. Theirs is an added helplessness and frustration. Jesus did not share this. His was a commanding personality, authoritative, powerful, his very look could subdue; a born leader of men. Only in his childhood did he know the other condition. No one listens to a little child. 'Small' people through their acceptance and love, can use this helplessness to grow in holiness. What is merely natural can become a sacrament of spiritual surrender.

It is born in on me more as the years go by, how profound is this theme of human helplessness and our loving acceptance of it. It is truly mystical. After long years in religious life, and having thought over and over again on its significance and the significance of the vows, I have come to see that it lies here. The vows of poverty and obedience, and to a certain extent the vow of chastity, though this stretches further out still, are a public, voluntary acceptance of a state of dependence and the helplessness that follows on it. Everyone by the sheer fact of his being human is in this condition willy-nilly; the religious, with eyes open, walks into a situation where this dependency and helplessness are going to be experienced in a fuller way.

For the religious, personal concerns are totally immersed in the concerns of the community. He cannot plan for himself, protect or provide for himself. He must be totally at the service of the community and in this submergence he is bound to suffer. This sort of helplessness, freely chosen, is the context in which he must live. Others may lawfully evade it whenever they can without harming others; the religious may not. Instinctive, largely inarticulate wisdom lies here. I think only those who really do take up this yoke, whether in religious life or out of it, learn by experience its rich, inner meaning; how it opens the heart to God and how he comes precisely in this helplessness. I doubt if in reality religious have to submit themselves to the yoke of obedience, to people and events any more than others; speaking generally I would think the opposite is true. But religious are supposed to have seen the meaning and, by their profession and fidelity to that profession, be showing others the value of what lies at hand, of that irksome reality ever present in their lives.

Deep in us all is the will to power, the will to control the world, to control people in order to serve our own ends. Our own ends may seem modest indeed, little more than self-preservation; nevertheless the ego standing behind this modest need has a rapacity far outstripping its claim. It is a mistake to think that it is only powerful personalities that are involved. The drive may be more obvious in them but it is there every

bit as much in the weak. Weakness itself becomes a manipu-
lative force. It is worth saying again at this point that temperament, force of personality or lack of it, have in themselves
nothing to do with holiness. In the kingdom of God there are
no such handicaps. The way to holiness for all of us requires
on our part an unselfish generosity in the efforts we must make
towards it in accepting the work of God, who reaches down to
our entrails to wrest us from our selfish selves.

In reality these two aspects intertwine. God is always working to bring us to an awareness and acceptance of our poverty,
which is the essential condition of our being able to receive
him, and the petty frustrations, the restrictions, humiliations,
the occasions when we are made to feel poignantly and dis-
tressingly hedged around, not in control of the world, not even
in control of that tiny corner of it we are supposed to call our
own, are his chosen channel into the soul. It is the one who
has learned to bow his head, to accept the yoke, who knows
what freedom is. There is so much that we must take whether
we like it or not; what I am urging is a wholehearted acceptance, a positive appreciation and choosing of this bitter ingredient of life.

No one who has read the gospel seriously can think that this
counsel of Jesus means a passive, cowardly 'I'm-a-door-mat-
walk-over-me' attitude. He always remains our example. He
accepted as none other ever can the essential poverty of the
human condition and the working out of that in everyday life.
He embraced it, but not without bitterness; he felt its sting
as we do. To surrender to the embrace of the Father in which
the human self joyfully, rapturously abdicates, is one thing; to
surrender to him in the human situation as it is, besmirched,
distorted by sin, is quite another matter, and Jesus felt the
horror and injustice, the outrage of it.

What is more, there is no sign of a passive acceptance of his
fate. We see a man of superb stature, with an unequalled
sense of mission and purpose, striving to fulfil that mission in
the teeth of all that raged against him. The more highly

developed the personality and sense of human dignity the more intensely will it feel the restrictions, injustices and indignities imposed. Many things will be experienced as the indignities they are which would readily and easily be accepted by others and not seen as such. Add to this developed personality a depth of spiritual insight which sees not merely a natural indignity but a sin against God, an outrage against one of his children and clearly the idea of meekness and humility prevalent among pious people finds no justification in the gospel. Jesus most certainly would not fit their image of the humble man.

Jesus surrendered to the forces he could not master but in a very real sense he laid down his life. He saw the awfulness of the sin committed, his horror and grief far transcended the personal outrage. No, the acceptance of dependency and helplessness is not a mealy-mouthed, grovelling attitude to life, to other people and to events, but a most brave, loving acceptance of what it means to be a human being in a fallen world. Only living faith can see this. It means really embracing Jesus, really believing in the Son of Man.

The more we try to understand what our Father asks of us and the more we try to put it into practice, the clearer it becomes that nothing is arbitrary, nothing just imposed from without; the commandments of Jesus belong to the very nature of things. What he asks fits our condition; his yoke is easy because it fits. Jesus, in his Father's name, asks nothing save that we be truly human and he shows us how. Would that human legislators had always understood this, would that they understood it even now! But because human fulfilment lies beyond the self and its egotism, which searches frantically within itself for its own immediate, comprehensible satisfaction, the acceptance of his teaching and of him, for he is his teaching, always demands humility, a bowing of one's neck to receive the yoke, an abdication of self in favour of him. This abdication is the essence of faith. It seems to me that wherever this acceptance of the human lot is found and in the measure that it is present, there is the Lord. An explicit acknowledgment of him is not necessary. In embracing what is truly human Jesus is embraced.

I suspect that this is often the case and there can well be more true acceptance of him in people who do not explicitly acknowledge him than in many who do, yet continually evade life and 'what is', often in his name. These others obey an inner urge which assures them there is meaning somewhere and that what they must do, the demand of their humanity, is to refuse to slump down in self but to surrender to life, bravely confronting it as it is and bowing before that which they cannot overcome.

The will to power is a tyrant we must strive to overcome. Of its nature it is a murderer and destroyer. To overcome it fully is not in our power; only God can uproot it, but we must do what we can all our life long. The disciple of Jesus, like his master, must be a cultivator and dispenser of abundant life. Every one of us has, in some way, power over others. There are those who have it lodged in their personality, the born leaders who exercise a natural authority by sheer force of personality. How careful such persons have to be. How full of reverence for the gift bestowed on them, how full of reverence for other people and all the stuff of which this world is made. They can never divest themselves of this influence even though they may long to do so after they have had to experience the perils to which it exposes them and others. What they have to do is to cultivate great purity of heart; they must want to know the truth about themselves, they must want to be shown the egotism, falsity, and lack of responsibility which pervade their lives.

I think only great self-knowledge, self-knowledge infused by God, can keep a naturally powerful person really humble in his dealings with others; self-knowledge and a most intense desire for God, which willingly sacrifices all self-advantage for his sake. A single end must be held steadily in view : God's holy will, which in practice means the true welfare of others. Jesus' tremendous gifts, his personal dynamism were laid at the feet of his Father. Never did he seek self-aggrandisement. We are shown in the gospel that he felt the allure of power, power to force men into the kingdom, to win them by false coin. He understood that such a manipulation, even though seemingly in the cause of God, would be a betrayal of God, a betrayal of his highest trust. Instead, as John tells us on the eve of the passion, the Father knew the heart of his Son and knew well that he could trust him with everything, could leave the welfare of his beloved children in his hands, because Jesus knew the Father's heart and all its loving will towards us.

Others, less gifted on the personal level, still have power in some form or other, by office, status, occupation, even by need. The sick and the dying, what power is in their hands, what power to make their little world move round them! There is not one of us, at whatever stage of life he be, who can afford to overlook this point or take it lightly. We have a murderer in our hearts. We have to seek him out and withstand him. Over and over again we need to recall to ourselves what it means to be a christian, indeed to be a man, for essentially the two are identical: a servant. To seek ourselves at the expense of another is to sin against our humanity and thus against God.

Failure to accept the innate poverty of our condition leaves us dominated by anxiety. Is it surprising, imperilled and threatened as we are? We are incessantly engaged, though we do not recognise the fact, in trying to ward off harm, to protect ourselves and hide our vulnerable condition from ourselves. Our relations with God are full of anxiety. We are bent on trying to placate a demanding God, one who is on the alert to find us at fault or, to put it more mildly, a God who won't be good to us until we have paid our full toll of holocausts and sin-sufferings, a God whom we cannot trust to be generous. Of course, this is unconscious and we are ready to convince ourselves that we are acting out of love and generosity. Only God can reveal to us the true state of things. We must be prepared to renounce this playing safe and learn to trust utterly in

God's goodness. We are God's dear children and must live as such. This means we must die to our self-protection, self-approval, self-sufficiency, and this means the death of every fear.

The activities on which we embark are not infrequently motivated by a desire to prove ourselves, to convince ourselves that we have resources within and are not the pitiable creatures that, deep down, we feel ourselves to be. Jesus himself was aware of this underlying, all-pervading fear in the heart of man and must have known its ground in himself. He saw the cheapness of life; men dropped to the earth dead no differently from sparrows. A building can suddenly topple and crush to death the men beneath; ruthless overlords rush on helpless men and massacre them. The fragility of life! Fevers carrying people off in an hour; here today and gone tomorrow. He was in continual contact with the maimed, the wrecked, the mad. He had the answer, not the explanation. You have a Father in heaven who knows. He loves you. Not a hair of your heads shall perish. What a superb guarantee, which if we could really make it our own would overcome our fear of life and death. You, as a person, are affirmed and guaranteed absolutely by the only one who can do so. Fear not, learn to trust the rocklike fidelity of your Father.

It often seems to me that what, from outside, seems to us sin and wickedness – violence, crime, drug-taking, sexual promiscuity – is not so in God's sight. Is it any more, I wonder, than the frantic screaming of a child in the frightening darkness of the night?

> An infant crying in the night:
> An infant crying for the light:
> And with no language but a cry.
> *In Memoriam*

We, privileged to know Jesus, can face the night and cry a name of endless comfort, 'Abba, Father'. But perhaps our faith is weak. Perhaps we pretend there is no darkness and therefore never know the need for this cry. Jesus knew it on the cross. He faced the darkness and met it with this cry. Or perhaps, faced with it, we have not the heart to cry; our faith fails and we deny our Father.

Blind trust is the only answer to our suffering state; a trust which leads us to accept with all our heart that God is our Father, Abba, and in that sureness go on without understanding. He has clearly shown us what we could not otherwise have known: that suffering is not his anger, it is not a sign that we have no part with him. On the contrary, we see that his own beloved, the sinless one, had an overwhelming share of suffering, and through him it is now transformed, becoming the means of fellowship with God. We cannot understand why suffering must be. Ultimately it rests on a divine decision, and this fact calls for trust on our part. Suffering of whatever kind is a little, partial death, a preview and reminder of what calls for the greatest act of faith of all, our physical dissolution. It is the fear of death, as the writer of Hebrews declares, which underlies all else and holds us in bondage. Destroy this and we are free men. This is what Jesus has done.

7

Love that is real

The love of God is inseparably bound up with love of our neighbour. Nothing is clearer in scripture. In fact, the two become one great commandment. 'To love the parent is to love his child' (1 Jn 5 : 1). It is as simple as that. Scripture does not place the weight of responsibility for our neighbour on the natural solidarity existing between men but solely on the fact that every one is like ourselves, God's child and the brother of Jesus. Only the grace of God, only transformation into Jesus, so that his love becomes my driving force, can enable me to love my neighbour as God wishes. 'Flesh and blood' cannot achieve this love. We are to love others as Jesus has loved us, no less, without discrimination, without limit, to the point of death. This does not simply mean that, if needs be, we must be prepared to lay down our lives for our neighbour whoever he be, but that daily we must be dying to our own selfish needs so as to care only for the welfare of others.

There is an enormous amount of neighbourliness in the world; kindness, thoughtfulness, readiness to help in difficulties, sympathy, generosity. One meets it everywhere. Nevertheless, the disciples of Jesus must exceed the demands of mere neighbourliness, wonderful though this is. Perfect love of our neighbour must be our aim, and this can flow only from a pure and selfless heart. We must begin with our inmost heart and this, in practice, means that charity begins at home.

We all know that it is relatively easy to be kind and neighbourly to those who don't press too closely on us, who are distanced from us to some extent. It is far more difficult to be always loving those with whom we live or rub shoulders with day after day. We all know the philanthropist, the zealot for the rights of the third world, who is harsh, critical and lacking in thought for those at home. A great deal of what we call charity may be self-love, satisfying a need in myself rather than pure seeking of my neighbour's good. I may want an outlet for my energies; I feel a need to be useful and important.

It is only when we are making sure that we are loving the neighbour whom we see that we may hope that our more far-reaching charity is pure. Love should flow in concentric circles with the centre at home. Possibly a contemplative, enclosed community such as the one I belong to is the most concentrated form of community you can get. We spend all our lives and the whole of our lives with the same few people, who have not been chosen by us. There will be some who are naturally congenial and some who are not, but this must make no difference to our love. Our Lord did not tell us we were to love only those whom we liked, but everyone without distinction. Unless we are constantly watchful and unless we have faced the truth about ourselves, we are bound to discriminate.

It can easily happen that we pass for very kind people, ever ready to lend a hand or do a good turn, and in our own heart we may think we are. But there will be one or two left out of this benevolent radiance. We shall be courteous to them, for we must not spoil the image we have of ourselves as charitable persons, but we shall be critical, ready to find fault in a discreet way, ready to use them as scapegoats. We shall find it hard to be fair in judgment where they are concerned. We shall come up with rational explanations of why we think as we do, but if we were really honest we would have to admit that in some way these people cut us down to size. In some way they challenge and threaten us. They may seem to undervalue us, perhaps are critical of us, and this makes us feel insecure. We don't like feeling like this so we must find some way of destroying these people – not literally but in so far as

they have power over us. We pull them down in our estimation or keep them severely at a distance. Even the heathen
can love those who love them, as our Lord says. His disciples
must love their enemies and do them good. Few of us have
enemies but we all have those who hurt us in one way or
another and we can be refusing our love to these. Because we
are good people we don't do outrageous things and therefore
our consciences are kept untroubled. We fail to see the great
importance of these small acts of injustice, or attitudes of
rejection which we hold. They are sin and come between us
and God. To leave one person out of our love is proof positive
– we need no other – that our love for others is not really
pure, not the love of Jesus. Our own self will be involved in
one way or another. It has always seemed to me that what
we experience in our form of community life is exactly the
same as we would anywhere else in the world, only more concentrated. We have the same dangers and the same struggles.

Two books, written within ten years of one another, impressed me deeply with the painful realisation that much of
what we think of as goodness and charity is merely the instinct
for survival operative among us. In *The Forest People* and *The
Mountain People* the anthropologist, Colin Turnbull, shares
with us a truly shattering experience, an experience which
shook, if not destroyed, his faith in humanity, humble, loving
man though he shows himself to be.

He spent several years living with the pygmies in the forests
of Uganda, accepted by them and studying their social behaviour. He found them a delightful people and their way of
life almost idyllic. Already, he claims, he had learned the
meaning of love from his parents and here among the forest
people he found it exemplified. The forest was their home and
their benevolent mother supplying them with all they needed.
Their God too was beneficent and the forests often rang with
his praises. In the forest, within the community, they could
stand up to sorrow and disaster, though outside it similar
disasters would disorientate them. They seemed a people with-

out evil : kind, gentle, considerate, trusting, mild in punishment, so peaceable that they experienced no need of an authoritative figure; all was agreed by common discussion and consent.

It seemed like Eden but a discerning mind could see the cracks. One or two of the people we meet have all the makings of rogues, and in different circumstances would have become so. Here it paid to be good and would have been death to be bad. On the other hand, there are others who, we judge, would maintain their standards anywhere regardless of circumstances.

They are a hunting people and a high community co-operation was absolutely essential for survival; to be excommunicated from the tribe meant certain death. We put down the book with a feeling of nostalgia . . . how beautiful! And yet there is a lingering question.

The answer meets us with brutal force in the later book. This likewise concerns a hunting tribe, the Ik, but one uprooted not many years before from its natural environment. Presumably for the same reasons as the Pygmies they too had a high standard of 'moral' behaviour when pursuing their nomadic, hunting existence. Wrenched from it, established in barren mountains which they were to farm, dependent on rains that did not come, subjected to famine, these people disintegrated with frightening rapidity. Of these, the author could only say 'I learnt not to hate them'.

He paints a terrible picture of what man is like when reduced to the level of concern for mere survival. There is no question of evil for evil's sake; there is no hatred because there is no love; just a heartless, uncaring concentration on self which is the nearest picture to hell we could imagine. Turnbull looks around desperately for some signs of humanity and goodness and finds them in a tiny few who, in spite of the horror and degradation all around them, recall the values of former times and maintain them.

The author wants us to see that under cover of our civilised ways and our social codes, the same self-centredness operates. If our society were to break down would not the same thing happen to us? We have seen many instances of this in our lifetime and seen too that a few can and do continue to love. This alone can be called true love, love that brings no reward other than itself, a love that believes all, goes on hoping and endures to the end. It is salutary to think this over. The reflection will keep us humble and mistrustful of ourselves. When we leave one person out of our love, or commit one act of unkindness, we are revealing that our so-called love is only there because it pays. When it doesn't pay it goes.

All our activities in this world should have as goal the forming of community. The building of this world, the effort to make it a better place to live in, our individual works and enterprises, all must have this goal in view, otherwise they depart from God's order. Community does not just happen, it has to be worked for, whether it be the community of the family or any community whatsoever. A community is not just a group living together. It is persons in communion and can never be built except on self-sacrifice.

I expect that most of us, at the outset, have approached community, whether of marriage or religious life, with the expectation of what we are going to get out of it, though this egotism would not be conscious. Community is there for our benefit, the other or others must give to us, love us, support us. Then we have to learn that this is not so. We have to give ourselves completely, sacrifice our own interests, be prepared to pour in all we have and are even though we seem to get nothing in return. It is only in this way that we can, in fact, gain the benefit of community, which is primarily growth as a person.

Jesus reiterated the great profession of dedication to God in the old testament. Who could understand its implications as he? 'You shall love the Lord your God with all your heart, and with all your soul and with all your strength, and with all your mind : and your neighbour as yourself' (Lk 10 : 27). If

E

we ponder these words we are impressed by the totality of the love demanded, the wholeness of the gift. This, I think, is the significance of consecrated virginity. Physical virginity of itself means nothing, what matters is spiritual virginity, this wholeness and totality. Now every christian is called to this spiritual virginity, implied in his baptismal consecration. He has to belong to God body and soul. Some are called to reach this in marriage, others in a single life in the world, others in a state of consecrated celibacy. The means are different, the end is the same. Indeed only certain of the means are different, most are identical. No one can attain it save by the constant effort to love at the expense of self, a constant disregard of self for the sake of others. Marriage and sexual love do not automatically lead to maturity and neither does abstention. Only love brings us to maturity. A consecrated chastity that does not flower in personal maturity and love is a travesty.

When someone, at our Lord's invitation, makes a vow of perpetual celibacy, they are saying 'I believe that you will bring me to perfect fulfilment apart from the normal means'. To undertake this risk without a divine call would be presumption, but when it is in answer to a divine invitation the renunciation implies a tremendous act of faith. What has to be borne in mind is that it is only the use of one's sexual powers that is to be sacrificed, not one's sexuality, that is, all that goes to make one either man or woman. To insist on giving God more than he asks, to insist on sacrificing other, essential means of growth such as real relationships with other people, is presumption. God won't work miracles. He expects us to do all we can to grow to full maturity through the use of all he has given us, so as to make our love of him and others all the richer. The consecrated virgin is meant to proclaim to the world that God and God alone is the supreme fulfilment of the human heart. She is a sign pointing to the summit which all must reach. An end is not reserved for her to which others may not attain. The end is the same for all but she, by what she becomes, must point clearly to that end.

Love is its own reward. If we love we grow in love and can receive more love. The world will not be transformed by great social schemes, important though these may be, but by individual men, women and children learning to love those nearest to them, divesting themselves of themselves in order to give themselves to others. Only thus can God take possession of his world.

8

Full of Light

We cannot love our neighbour, we cannot serve our Lord purely, unless we know ourselves. 'The eye is the lamp of the body. So, if your eye is sound, your whole body will be full of light; but if your eye is not sound, your whole body will be full of darkness. If then the light in you is darkness, how great is the darkness' (Mt 6 : 22–23). The heart has its eye, an eye that must be kept clean and healthy. Too often our inward sight is defective and hence our heart is in darkness. We do not see as we should see, we are blinded by our selfishness. Profound, searching self-knowledge is infused, it flows from the direct contact of holiness and truth with the inmost heart, but it is our duty to do all we can to gain what light we can, whether it be an understanding of God as he has revealed himself or an understanding of ourselves. What we do is all-important as a preparation to receive the light which will come direct from him. Even what we can do ourselves is the effect of his grace and without him we are all darkness.

Knowledge of self means knowledge of our emotions. A human being must judge, decide, act, according to reason, not according to emotion. Emotions have a great role to play in our functioning as human beings but only when they are well-harnessed. If they are not harnessed they will run away with us, and the direction will not be Godwards. They must be our servants, we must not be their slave. Most good people of reasonable maturity do not allow themselves to be carried away by emotions into more obvious wrongdoing, or if they do so they know it and are sorry. But it will be extraordinary if we are not being governed by them nearly all the time in secret ways, unless we have taken the matter seriously to heart and are determined to know ourselves, cost what it may.

It is costly, humiliating, and frightening but there is no answer to this except trust in our Lord who loves us just as we are. I do not think we can ignore the science of psychology. This is not to say it is essential and it can certainly be overdone. It is dismaying to see the way psychological counselling is identified with spiritual direction, as though a thorough knowledge of psychology, if such a thing were possible, plus a little spirituality is adequate equipment for spiritual direction. A lot of time can be wasted on interesting experiments on one's fascinating self – getting to know oneself, it would be said – which would be better employed getting on with life. Unless this sort of thing really leads to a change of heart, a more careful and conscientious fulfilment of one's obligations and a more selfless love for others, it is useless.

Nevertheless, the rejection of psychological knowledge, guidance and help, is hardly a healthy sign. Some of us are quite ready to prescribe it for others but not ready to accept it for ourselves. We don't want to have to face ourselves and have our inner securities shaken; we had far rather let sleeping dogs lie. But surely if we want God we should crave for this light, we should be ready to let the pathetic securities which we have built up in ourselves be overthrown, because we do not want to rely on ourselves but on God. This is the challenge of faith. The science of psychology is a feature of our times, and can we ignore it? To be true to our humanness means accepting these human helps. In the same way with science at our elbow it would be foolish and presumptuous to start asking God for miracles to cure what modern medicine can deal with.

We need to reckon with our subconscious. Lots of things have been pushed down there because the facing of them would hurt too much. If we want fellowship with Jesus we must be ready to retrieve some of this lost material, otherwise we can never be whole, never have our soul in our hands to give ourselves to God. We shall continue to be controlled by these hidden impulses and enslaved. As regards the unconscious, is it not enough to know of its presence so that we are not tricked? Is there any justification for trying to get at this mysterious area of being? Surely it fulfils its function left to itself and is better left to itself. It is meant to be unconscious – provided we are aware of its existence.

Our Lord knew of the power our emotions have and how they deflect us from maturity. There is no question of his condemning them. He took them for granted and sanctioned them. He recognised and accepted the deep, emotional bonds binding people to one another. He worked miracles at the plea of grief-stricken parents, the sorrow of the bereaved distressed him and called forth his compassion and desire to help. A delicate courtesy prompted him to take the child he had cured by the hand and give him back to his father, clearly recognising the bond between them. He took for granted parental love which would never refuse its child what it needed, and the forgiving father called to mind the attitude of his own Father. The story of Cana clearly demonstrates the happy, trustful relationship between him and his mother; he provided for her at his death. But he was insistent that these bonds should not hinder us from growing up and fulfilling our destiny.

As a young boy he was ready to detach himself from his parents at the call of his destiny. In his mature life he resisted the pressure of his relatives. Because he was different, because his attitudes, his way of seeing things and his behaviour were different from their own, they were disturbed and uneasy. The only explanation they could think of was that he had gone crazy. He was moved by a spirit they could not understand. And is this not always happening? It takes courage to break free, to pursue one's independent course, to be true to oneself and one's destiny. Merely the lack of understanding on the part of those we love can cause suffering, let alone their hostility and rejection. It would not be difficult to succumb.

Jesus knew the force of the conflict and that anyone who would follow him closely and share his spirit, would feel the sword of separation cutting him off from his own kin and that society which is his wider kin. 'I have come to set a man against his father, and a daughter against her mother, and a daughter-in-law against her mother-in-law, and a man's foes will be those of his own household. He who loves father or mother more than me is not worthy of me' (Mt 10 : 35-37). It is not merely a question of being ready to leave those we love to follow our Lord – this is not asked of the majority of his disciples – but all are called to the freedom and detachment he is speaking of.

We crave passionately for the security of belonging to and being accepted by others. This acceptance seems to validate and its refusal to undermine us. Unconsciously, to a great measure, we tend to build ourselves up on the good opinion others have of us and, on the other hand, wilt under their disapproval. Behind this lies the fear of our own poverty. Fear drives us here and there in a desperate search for reassurance. The only answer is trustful acceptance of our innate littleness, sure of our Lord's love for us. If we accept, if we are sure of his love, then we do not mind discovering more and more of our inner weaknesses. We know we have an answer in him, we don't have to find our own answer. He is the only one we have to please and we please him by trusting him with our sinfulness.

We long too to relieve ourselves of the responsibility for the risks involved in running our own lives, in making our own decisions. We feel, unconsciously, that this can be shifted onto the shoulders of the collective and then we are safe from blame. The family, a religious order, the church as an institution— these can be the focus for identification. Our poverty is covered over in this identification. We do not realise how unfree we are. Jesus wants us to share the freedom to stand before his Father, obedient to his will, flexible, on our toes. The passion for security can make us unbendable, refusing to change, clinging to structures and attitudes now outworn. On the other hand, equally immature instincts can drive us to unwise change, from one state of life to another, from one community to another, to a craze for experience and fulfilment.

Many, many times I have heard it said by spiritual directors that what people need above all is encouragement. It is certainly true if properly understood. The encouragement we need is to be led to the Father of compassion who is always ready to give, so as to make him our total security. But what we usually mean by encouragement is a pat on the back and congratulations for our spiritual performance. We want to be assured of our own innocence and spiritual achievement, and injudicious assurance of this kind is harmful and leads to complacency. It should not be given unless there is real knowledge of the person concerned, whereas one need never hesitate to assure anyone whatsoever of God's tender love for them. Jesus would never foster our illusions. To feel we have got somewhere, that we are spiritual people, is the most cherished possession of the devout, and this has to be abandoned. Imprudent counsel can hinder rather than help. A striking example of this is to be found in a life of St Bernadette of Lourdes, *A Grain of Wheat* by Margaret Trouncer. It concerns Mère Vauzou, the one time novice mistress of the saint.

By any impartial judgment, this woman had treated Bernadette abominably, in a way totally at variance both with our Lord's teaching and with common humanity, even if it could be said, which is doubtful, that she acted with a pure motive. Constantly she displayed a marked antipathy towards her and never lost an opportunity for a snub. Even when the child lay deadly sick in the infirmary, this woman, visiting the other patients, deliberately passed her by. It seems she was consumed by jealousy for this peasant girl, the object of an attention and veneration which she coveted for herself. The blessed Virgin had shown remarkably bad taste and lack of judgment in passing over the well-born Mère Vauzou for the sake of a wretched peasant.

As the posthumous fame of her former charge grew and the question of her canonisation was raised, Mère Vauzou's conscience, we are told, began to prick her. Travelling in the south of France she seized the opportunity to visit a priest renowned for holiness and discernment of spirit; 'he was very kind and his aim was to restore confidence in troubled souls'. She emerged from a long conversation with him and from confession, beaming with happiness, and told her companion : 'I'm very happy to have seen that holy man . . . I was frightened that I had been too severe to ma Soeur Marie Bernard. That was tormenting me. I told him why I acted as I did. Père Jean completely reassured me, and now I am very much at peace'.

How we can delude ourselves! This priest could only know what she told him and clearly she put herself in the best light. The members of her own community, those who lived with her, could have given her better counsel. As it was, the burden of her conscience was removed by the authority figure, she need worry no more, the agony of uncertainty was gone, the vote was in her favour. She could reassure herself; the torment was not due to guilt but to scruples. Surely she should have been faced with the enormity of her sin and made to assume full responsibility for it, and only then offered the certainty of God's complete forgiveness. It was not with the peace of Christ that she left him but with a false peace, her supposed innocence unimpaired, her spiritual image still shining. Yet here was the opportunity God must have been contriving so that she might face the truth, accept her sinfulness and begin to give herself to our Lord.

Most good people are ready to make general statements about themselves. 'I'm a poor thing', 'I'm a good-for-nothing', 'I'm no saint'. It is easy to do so. It is quite another matter to face up to a specific fault; this means we have to do something about it. The course you have been pursuing in regard to X which, you maintain, is prompted only by highest motives is, in reality, motivated by jealousy. How much harder to take, humbling in its self-revelation and demanding a total change of course. A vague, general awareness of not being as good as we would like to be gets us nowhere, we need to get down to facts.

We choose how much we see and how much we do not see. The choice is barely conscious but it is choice none the less. At the moment in question we might be in good faith convinced that we are doing right. But the point is that somewhere along the line, perhaps very far back, perhaps only one step behind, there has been a decision to see no further. It may have gone something like this – though in a side whisper not to be heard by ourselves – 'I'm not prepared to go *that* far; I never bargained for *that* sort of giving'. Or, 'I simply must cling to my securities. If they are taken away I shall be destroyed'. For some of us the decision was taken long ago.

Can it ever be undone? Yes, if we really wish. This is part of what conversion means. Unless we choose to see and are willing to accept the pain and demands of seeing we shall go on in our blindness. If it is not dissipated in this life it will be so at death when we stand before the Son of Man and see ourselves as we are. He is 'judge of the living and the dead' not in the sense that he assumes the role of a judge appraising the conduct of our lives, but in the sense that our only value lies in our likeness to him.

It is not our weaknesses and failures that matter but our refusal to recognise them as such, our persistence in hiding them from ourselves or in giving them other names. To recognise that we have made wrong choices and that those choices persist, in that we are living with their consequences, opens us to God and the consequences then are no obstacle to his love.

'Lord, that I may see!' must be the constant cry of the heart that wants God. It is the cry for purity of heart, the single virginal heart which will see the face of God in the way it can be seen in this life.

9

As men who are free

To be truly living as Jesus wants us to live, at each moment we must be able to answer the question, 'What am I doing and why am I doing it?' This means we must have thought out and continue to rethink the principles which are to be the springs of our choices and actions, and these principles must be those which governed our Lord's life. There is really not one moment in life when we are not asked to choose, and the choice will always be between God or ourself. Half the time we are not choosing but drifting along on whatever current is under us, acting on impulse, through routine, conforming to convention, answering expectations. This is not human living.

Others can help in our education; we can ask and receive advice, but ultimately it is we who decide and choose and the responsibility is ours alone. No one can live our life for us. A careful reading of the gospel reveals the gravity of our responsibility for the way we live our life on earth. Every careless word has its consequences; our thoughts, words, actions, the secret intent of our hearts, all of these are to be answered for with no possibility of evasion.

We can never excuse ourselves for wrongdoing by appealing to authority and to the example of others. It is easy enough to think that, because so-and-so does this or that it is all right for us to do so too. We can be running our lives or large areas of them on this assumption without being aware of it. We are too lazy and don't care enough to come to grips with life. Not even ecclesiastical authority can take away the burden of responsibility. Mostly, for the sake of the common good and because Jesus asks it of us, we bow our heads and obey, but knowing what we are doing and why. We are choosing to obey having looked carefully over the issues, and are not acting in blind subservience and craving for security. We may well think that what is ordered is foolish, perhaps harsh and something our Lord would not enjoin, but unless sin is involved and real harm to others then we are confident that our Lord wants us to obey. He, and Paul after him, urge upon us this ready submission to others – a mature, intelligent submission, the act of a free man.

On the other hand, we cannot excuse ourselves for having inflicted harm on others or having committed any other moral fault, pleading that we were merely carrying out orders. We have all read horrifying instances of this in the mid-century. It is a common human failing and experiments have shown just how common it is. Few there are who will not hurt another if commanded to do so even when the commands are not accompanied by threat. Authority, using plausible arguments, gives directives; the majority blindly obey.

One who is close to our Lord has an instinct for what is right and is free, in the measure of his closeness, from the influence of accepted custom. He looks at our Lord, not at what others think and do. A simple incident will illustrate this. Someone I know was present in a workshop when the phone rang. The apprentice answered it. It was a client, asking why an article sent into the shop some weeks before had not been returned. The apprentice passed on the message to the foreman, who was there in the room. 'Oh, tell him we are very sorry for the delay but we are waiting for a spare part that has not come yet. We can't get on without it'. Now, both the foreman and the apprentice knew this was a lie. The object was there in front of them, no spare part was needed, it had been overlooked. The boy went back to the phone and delivered the message exactly as given. Later, the onlooker said to him :

'Don't you get into the habit of telling lies. You knew that was a lie'. The boy excused himself, 'but Mr X told me to say it'. 'I don't care who told you to say it, it was a lie and we mustn't tell lies'.

The readiness to tell the hypocritical, kindly lie to save trouble; readiness to evade customs and other taxes; misuse of working hours when the results cannot be assessed; gladly taking advantage when fares have not been collected, these and similar immoral actions are alien to the disciples of Jesus, who are limpid and incorruptible. It is with them as Jesus wanted, their simple 'yes' is yes and their 'no' is no.

Too many would-be spiritual people who say they want nothing but God are casual in their behaviour. Religious are some of the worst offenders, slow to pay their bills, ready to get everything as cheaply as they can regardless of the consequences to others, expecting and demanding privileges. It is the daily acts of goodness that count. They are unspectacular yet shine like light in a dark world, revealing to that world what goodness is; infinitely more important than the ability to expound theology, to write movingly about the ways of God, more important than devotional exercises.

We must keep on reviewing our conduct, holding it up to the light of the gospel, really wanting the light to show where we are wrong. It is no use putting in a lot of time for prayer and making a thing of the spiritual life if our dealings with others are not characterised by scrupulous honesty, justice, kindness. Unless we are on the watch, just because we are basically lazy and self-seeking, we shall take the line of least resistance and all sorts of dishonesties and injustices will vitiate our life. They won't disturb our conscience because they are not glaring, but they are equally destructive of love.

There must be occasions in the life of many lay people when the issues are much greater than a little inconvenience, loss of status, the scorn of our fellows, when it is perhaps a question of losing one's job, a loss affecting not only oneself but the family. To be honest, scrupulously honest in business may well involve great loss in this crooked world. I pass over in respect-ful silence such a test as this, it has never come my way.

Such a test confronted St Thomas More with its dire demands. Few have his moral integrity and courage. Thomas had every excuse for yielding. After all, every one else was doing so, the wise and the good included; why should he be right and they wrong? Surely they knew better than he. And was there not confusion and doubt concerning the issues them-selves? In the play, *A Man for All Seasons*, Thomas replies to his young son-in-law, Roper, 'I'd trust myself to *you* but not to your principles'. See the contrast between these two. Thomas, fully aware of the corruption of the papacy, still saw it as so fundamental to the church that he was prepared to die to uphold it. Many others, up to the time of testing, affirmed its importance. Presumably they proclaimed their firm belief in its divine institution. Events showed clearly that this was not belief, not conviction held firmly from within, but a mere point of view superimposed from without; let public opinion change and it too would change.

For Thomas and a few others likewise ready to die, it was not a mere point of view but a deep conviction, their own. Roper, and others like him (do not we belong here?) thought they were acting on principle but the ease with which they could swing around when it was convenient, reveals that they were not. Probably we all have illusions of this kind. We may well think we have deeper convictions than we really have. If we were in different circumstances, open to different influ-ences and ideologies, how much would we know from within? Would we hold to our conviction though everyone else thought otherwise, even without threat save that, perhaps, of being at odds with our companions, not being wholly acceptable to them? A more careful appraisal of our daily conduct might bring us many surprises.

10

And it was very good

It is in this world, through its proper exploitation, that God's children grow towards him. Each of us has been given abilities and these must be deployed responsibly, joyfully. God's activity mingles with our activity and does not stand apart from it. His mystical activity comes into play in this properly human sphere, in the throb of life. A disciple of Jesus must give a total affirmation to human values. The dying to this world must never be understood as an opting out, a denial of those values. It is not to the world as such that we have to die but to our self-centredness. It is true that we have to transcend this world and its values but we can only transcend them in the measure that we have made them our own.

We have to work to make the world more radiant with God. He positively wills that man should explore the universe and try to master it. Man grows by doing so. Inevitably he is going to blunder, over-reach himself with unhappy, perhaps disastrous consequences. But God is not going to blame him for his mistakes. God is not 'angry' at man's attempting these things. On the contrary he is pleased. It is nature that does not forgive, rather than God. He looks with immense compassion on the sufferings which follow in the wake of man's mistakes; these sufferings, seen as part of the human lot and bravely born, become the cross of Christ. Surely the disciple of Jesus does not stand in the wings, coldly disapproving and ready to point the finger of scorn when things go wrong. Rather he should be involved, understandingly, sympathetically. Let him make sure that in all his own activities there is nothing selfish, but that in all things he is seeking the good of others. This is the best thing he can do to ensure that others do likewise.

An essential ingredient of being human is that we are creatures of history as Jesus was. This means that, like him, we are inevitably conditioned and limited by our times, by the structures and thought processes of the age in which we live. Because of his cultural situation our Lord was unable, perhaps disinclined, to extend his mission beyond the frontiers of Israel in his lifetime. What potentialities might have lain dormant in him for want of opportunity? None of us can evade the consequences of being in history and we have to embrace this necessity as God's will.

God, for us, is in this particular era with its advantages and disadvantages. Whether we like it or not we must live in our contemporary world and must love it precisely because it is God's will for us. We might well prefer the simpler forms of life of earlier days, we may fear and detest excessive technology, we may feel threatened and oppressed by what is going on and are powerless to prevent. I don't suppose our Lord enjoyed being in an occupied country at a time when the highest authority was not partial to Jews. I expect he too felt threatened. But we cannot opt out. We have to go on playing our part, or rather living our lives in this age, not trying to hang on to an age that has gone. To do that is to deny part of the human condition, and in the measure that we do it, we withdraw from Jesus, who embraced our condition as his *raison d'être*.

We must recognise that being a man means being in evolution. Man and his world have to change. We must be ready to see that even ways of thinking about God, credal expressions, not only may but must change. To deny that they must is to deny that man is in history. Here is a vast area for loving sacrifice which religious people may overlook or not exploit as they should. Otherwise in the name of religion they may well become the opponents of change and champions of the past. In doing this they deny the Lord of history.

Any spirituality which would demand in God's name a denial of pleasure, that would seek to escape from the material and slight the needs of the body, is not christian. A christian joyfully accepts his bodiliness, knowing that he can go to God only through his body and that God comes to him through his body. He believes, because Jesus has told him so, that God is his loving Father who knows his needs and has given him the good things of this world for his wellbeing and happiness. The lingering guilt feelings of an older generation, due to the Jansenistic elements in their early religious training, must be seen for what they are, mere feelings, and ignored. God takes delight in our delight in the good things he has given us, goods of the senses, of the mind and heart.

From the earliest ages of the church, a false asceticism has tried to impose itself, an asceticism deriving more from hatred of the body, a hatred born of pride and fear, than from the love of God. Nowhere in the gospel shall we find justification for such an attitude. Jesus saw everything as flowing from the Father's heart. Behind the splendour of ephemeral flowers and grasses lies the Father's creating love. He took for granted that men and women married. One of his favourite images for the happiness of heaven and its prelude in his kingdom on earth is a wedding feast. The first of his great signs as John describes it took place by special design at a wedding feast. Its symbolism was bound up with the wedding. A human occasion, and his own mother was there. We can be sure it was solid and earthy with no prudishness or 'Victorianism'. Wine flowed freely and spirits were high, so high that the steward knew they could get away with poor wine towards the end of the party. Jesus did not take offence. He was part of it all.

As I write, Rembrandt's picture of the Jewish Bride is on my table. It is beautiful in its bodiliness, the body the vehicle of personal love and surrender, the very symbol of our surrender to God. The husband has his left arm around his wife's

F

shoulder, his right hand is laid upon her breast. Her right hand has strayed instinctively to her womb, whilst her other has met her husband's over her heart. He is absorbed in her but she is not looking at him, rather she is gazing before her, absorbed in what this act must mean for her. Gravely, wonderingly she ponders on the depth of trust and abandonment demanded of her and the fruitfulness that will follow. True marriage is the image of our relations with our Lord.

Quite obviously Jesus enjoyed food and drink. He calmly quotes the gossip about him : 'they say, "Behold, a glutton and a drunkard" ' (Mt 11 : 19). Such a censorious attitude towards his simple enjoyment must have hurt. Not only that, he realised that his attitude to the ordinary pleasures of life robbed him of spiritual authority in the eyes of the religious people of his day. John the ascetic, with his hairshirt, severe fasting and estrangement from the world, they could understand, but not this fellow who seemed to live too rooted in our workaday world. A man of God should be an ascetic, not one of the ordinary folk, doing as others do. Jesus refused to change his attitude even though by so doing he might have won them. But this would have been to betray the truth and his mission. What a profound lesson lies here !

When challenged about fasting, that John's disciples fast but yours don't, he had this answer : 'Can the wedding guests mourn whilst the bridegroom is with them? The days will come when the bridegroom will be taken away from them, and then they will fast' (Mt 9 : 15). Again the image of a wedding, the joy of marriage and its disruption when the bridegroom is taken away, proof of his simple acceptance of life as it is. What Jesus is saying here is that the fast of those who love him, who have centred their lives on him, is precisely his absence as regards the senses. This is the only fast that matters in God's eyes. Their senses must fast as that of a bride deprived of her husband. We can call it the fast of faith.

Faith is a fast, it is a refusal to put anything in the place of God, and an acceptance of the consequent sense of deprivation. Faith refuses to seek the sensible assurances our nature craves for, and insists on looking beyond, reaching out to him who cannot be savoured in this life. For one who has given his heart to our Lord there is a perennial fast while this life lasts. It is in this context I think that we must look for christian asceticism. Christian asceticism has its roots in love of Jesus, not in fear of the body and the world at large.

For the fast of faith to be real, for the christian to maintain a hunger for God, a God who does not satisfy his senses, he must take care not so to encompass himself with the good things of this world that his need for God is not experienced. If his desire for God is genuine, and we must not confuse real desire with a feeling or emotion, then he will want to express it in concrete forms. Outward expressions strengthen the inner disposition. Hunger for God has to be worked for. It is a sustained act of choosing under the influence of grace. The lack of religious emotion, if such there be, may well form part of the fast of faith. Hunger for God is born of faith not of feeling. It is maintained by the exercise of faith. There would be something incongruous in a person insisting that they want God, yet never depriving themselves of anything, always having everything they want when they want.

Christian austerity aims at freedom and reverence; it ensures that we receive God's gift of pleasure in an ever more personal way. A christian is dedicated to love and life; love of God and his neighbour, assuring for himself and his neighbour an increasing abundance of life. But we have a murderer in our hearts who would destroy not only ourselves but others also, and we cannot ignore him. Now although we can truly say that a christian's aim must always be positive, yet to maintain this positive aim he must to some extent adopt a negative one. Thus the negative becomes positive, it is at the service of life. We cannot seek God always and serve our neighbour with a disinterested love until we have looked at ourselves, discerned where we are selfishly seeking ourselves, and then positively denied this self-seeking and worked against it. We can go on blithely thinking we are seeking God and serving our neighbour when all the while we are seeking ourselves and our own satisfaction.

Pleasure and satisfaction accompany every proper human activity. This is God's loving ordinance for us, both to ensure that we fulfil our functions, activate our potentialities and grow, and also to make our earthly life as happy as possible. The trouble is that in our selfishness we seek pleasure at the expense of love and duty. As we have a passion for power so we have a passion for pleasure and satisfaction, whether of the senses or of the spirit. Unless we take careful stock of this, without realising it we shall become enslaved and at the mercy of our likes and dislikes. Mastery and control do not drop from the skies; we have to discipline ourselves for the sake of love. There must be times when, to ensure our freedom, to ensure that we can say 'no' to ourselves, we must deny ourselves some perfectly legitimate pleasure. We have a right to it but for love's sake, to ensure that we can love, we deny ourselves.

Moderate, sustained ascetical practices are of far greater value than spurts of a more drastic kind. Enthusiasm can carry us over the more spectacular feats – night vigils, severe fasts – but enthusiasm doesn't last. It last as long as we get a kick out of these things and when the kick goes so does the enthusiasm. It is far better to have established simple, prudent rules for what to eat, how long to sleep and so on, and keep to them. Better moderate, unspectacular discipline than outbursts of sensational penance which do little more than gratify our sense of having done something worthwhile. We are not likely to get much satisfaction from our small but constant acts – on the contrary we are likely to feel ashamed of their inadequacy – but if they are kept up for the love of our Lord, to express in tangible form that we want God to be our heart's love, they are of great value and efficacy.

The danger with immoderate penance is that it diverts us from what matters most, the continual waiting on God to see what he wants of us : fidelity in this duty, kindness to that person we don't want to be kind to, application to the work we are set when we want a change, and so on. To undertake special acts of penance can give us the illusory sense that we are generous people, that God matters a lot to us, when all the time we are struggling to keep him and his demands out of earshot.

At the beginning of our life for God we have to be tougher on ourselves, especially if we have indulged ourselves and had everything pretty much as we want it. We are not going to get out of this bad habit of self-indulgence without a struggle and our earnestness in this will be proof of the genuineness of our desire to live for God. When we have acquired a measure of control then we can allow ourselves greater freedom. If our hearts belonged wholly to God we could be completely free and happy in the use of everything God has given us, but until we are we have to watch jealously lest craving for our own pleasure blunts our earnestness in seeking God.

This watchfulness over the desire for pleasure and satisfaction must extend to spiritual things as well. Bodily indulgence can humiliate us but spiritual indulgence foments pride. We may, at times, derive immense satisfaction from our spiritual duties, at other times not. Or there may be some spiritual activities which give us satisfaction and others that don't. For instance, we may get much more satisfaction attending a shared prayer session than we do from mass. What matters is that we never allow such satisfaction to become a motive force. It can do so without our realising it. We are not asked to reject the delight we might feel in our devotional activities, of course not, but we must not give this delight a significance it has not got. Because we get a greater sense of God's presence at a prayer meeting than at mass or in silent prayer, it does not mean that God is in fact more for us in the prayer meeting and that we are justified in opting for that form of spiritual activity rather than for those which give no satisfaction. Perseverance in spiritual duties whether pleasurable or not is of supreme importance. To take up this or that because it pleases, because it is interesting, and to drop it when the interest goes; to pray when we feel like it and not when we don't, is to make a farce of prayer and to use God for our self-indulgence.

The most valuable form of asceticism, because it is the actual exercise of love, is the patient acceptance of the hardships and sufferings of life. For every good, responsible person there is a large measure of suffering which he takes in his stride, hardly adverting to it – it is part of life. Nevertheless it is just this hidden cross, patiently shouldered day after day, that gradually wears down our selfishness. It is the more precious in that it is hidden even from ourselves and does not flatter our pride. Monotony is one such cross.

Everyone from childhood upwards has to learn to take monotony if they would get anywhere. It seems an inescapable part of human existence, inescapable that is if we are true to our human condition. There must come a time for each responsible person when options are closed, a way of life is chosen and perseverance in that way of life will be the actual expression of our dedication to God. Perhaps earlier generations did not feel the same irksomeness in monotony; nowadays there seems a resentment against it as though it should not be, as though our interest and enjoyment must be catered for at every turn, and as if when work becomes boring we were justified in abandoning one field of action for another. All that matters is our fulfilment, our satisfaction in what we do and accomplish. We may call it other names but honesty would make us admit that we are crassly self-seeking. It looks as if many religious calmly accept this attitude to monotony. It is only those who can persevere for a long time who will come to maturity. 'A rolling stone gathers no moss.' No matter how much we enjoy our work, and surely this is most desirable, there will be elements in it that test our endurance and patience over a long period.

No one claims that of itself suffering purifies, but suffering patiently and bravely borne plays an indispensable role in human development. God offers himself to us at every moment, in our joys as well as in our sorrows, nevertheless there is a sense in which he offers himself more intimately in suffering. It is because in difficulty and suffering our hearts can be more open to receive him. We are painfully aware of our limitations and our need. Suffering creates a loneliness which others cannot penetrate; our sense of emptiness brings the realisation that we can find no answer to the mystery of ourselves in this world. We are more likely to feel the need of a saviour and open our hearts to him.

Long-drawn-out suffering that carries with it no element of self-satisfaction can be a special channel of God's entry into our hearts. Living for a long time with a difficult person, which demands a constant effort to be loving and understanding; temperamental difficulties which dog our footsteps, overshadowing us even on our brightest days; perseverance in a dull, demanding job, not merely for the sake of it but because duty demands. Then the still deeper suffering of seeing those we love in pain; lingering illness; anxiety about those we love; anxiety about our means of livelihood, fear of losing our job; bereavement which leaves an aching void for the rest of life. It is not the spectacular occasion which really costs, the sort of thing that suddenly lifts us out of routine and gives us the opportunity for splendid courage. It is amazing to what heroic heights ordinary people attain in time of crisis. But does this tell us much about the moral stamina of those involved? People who show up splendidly in crises can prove self-centred and childish in the ordinary rough and tumble of life. If we are looking for real heroism, the sort of heroism Jesus displayed, then we are likely to find it in some very ordinary man or woman, getting on with the job of living, totally unaware that they are doing anything remarkable and completely without pretension.

We are only too ready to run from the quiet room where God is hidden, and where he gives himself in hidden ways, to the busy market-place where spiritual excitement is to be had. We can rush here and there, busy with this and that, throwing ourselves into project after project which has far more to do with self-gratification than the kingdom of God. If we want to love our Lord and our neighbour, we must acquire the habit of disregarding our likes and dislikes. When some choice is before us, when something irksome or distasteful comes our way, we must be able to say each time: 'All that matters is what God wants. What I feel or don't feel is of no consequence whatever. I don't matter, it is God that matters,' and most often in a concrete situation it will be 'it is others that matter, not I.'

It is by no means uncommon to find people making a cult of suffering in the name of spirituality. It is often a case of imagining one is the victim of persecution, when what is happening is that, convinced that suffering of this kind is a sure sign of great holiness, we are bringing it about. Much the same can be said of psychological suffering. True, when this is there and cannot be got rid of, it can become a putrifying agent, but only when we are trying to keep above it. The mistake is when we interpret this as spiritual suffering and take satisfaction in it. We think it is a sign of advancement and thus it becomes a treasured possession. Such creatures we are! Anything can be used to boost our poor selves. Secrecy is a key-word. Our Lord said we were to take care not to display our good works to the admiration of men, and we must be careful not to display them to ourselves. Once we start examining our suffering, the way we are bearing it, and congratulating ourselves, God can no longer use it. It ceases to be suffering.

So deeply ingrained in the christian tradition as it has come down to us is the fear of pleasure, particularly intense pleasure as in sex, that although common sense and innate wisdom now frees christians to accept it, nevertheless some guilt still remains. Perhaps it just means that we feel disqualified from real holiness. And perhaps for a Carmelite to be insisting that this deeply-rooted fear in the church's bloodstream is evil, seems ironic. Maybe someone will turn round and say 'Well, if you are so convinced that acceptance of the great pleasures of life is not only not incompatible with holiness but normally essential to it, why have you felt obliged to renounce them? It can't be right for some and not for others.'

The answer is simply one of vocation. Some are asked to renounce pleasures but this is abnormal and in itself dangerous. This renunciation is a form of ministry in the church whereby the rest of the family, whose vocation it is to go to God through the proper use of all these good things, may in fact use them purely in the service of love. Pleasure is precisely to urge us on to the fullness of life and this means to the fullness of love. Love and life are a greater good than all the pleasures in the world; the latter easily steal first place. The fact that some renounce them for the sake of life and love keeps the end clearly shining. Also, the particular function of contemplative religious demands this curtailment; they would get in the way of that function. No one can do everything, specialisations demands renunciations.

This renunciation in religious is only relative, not absolute. No one can renounce all pleasure, to do so would be to deny that one was human. We have an absolute need of pleasure. Apart from sex, where renunciation is total, it is only a matter of degree. What is more, intensity of pleasure is not proportionate to self-indulgence; self-indulgence can blunt the edge of pleasure, whereas self-discipline can sharpen it. Possibly we get more pleasure out of our little pleasures than others do from theirs. To become atrophied, shrivelled, petty through the rejection of the pleasures and delights God has strewn in our path, is an insult to love. He will not thank us for that.

11

That you may have life

Prayer is not just one function in life, not even the most important, it is life itself. We are only truly living, truly and fully human when our whole life is prayer. Our idea of prayer will depend on the idea we have of God. We may see God as a distant, almighty, though benevolent being, to whom we must in duty bound offer our worship, thanksgiving and petitions, coming before his throne at fixed times to acknowledge his rights over us and to pay him his dues. The rest of the time we get on with the business of living here on earth. We know he is looking on, ready to reward our good actions and reprove us for our bad. The reward consists of a credit mark against our name in heaven and the sum total of these credit marks will decide the degree of glory and happiness in heaven when we die. Or we may understand that as a reward for our good acts God gives us 'grace', a mysterious something that makes us strong and beautiful and pleasing to him. The more filled with grace we are when we die, the happier we shall be in heaven. This is caricature, no doubt, but possibly it comes nearer to the truth of our attitudes than we might care to admit.

In this context, prayer is a function in life and has very little to do with the rest of life. It ensures keeping on the good side of God. The truth is very different, and we learn the truth not from our poor, sinful hearts but from the revelation of Jesus. The teaching of the New Testament shows us God, not 'out there' but most intimately present in the very heart and blood pulse of our lives. What is more, he is not a great lord who

takes delight in the homage of his vassels and servants and is
affronted when these are denied; he isn't interested in himself
and his own advantage, he is only concerned with us and our
happiness, and this happiness is his happiness. He is obsessed
with us, wholly absorbed with caring for us; every detail of
our lives, every cell of our body is a matter for his concern –
our Lord tells us so. He has all the passionate, intense concern
of the most loving of parents. Specifically, his one aim is to give
us himself. This, as a simple statement, can mean little to us.
We have to take it on faith that this is the highest, ultimate
blessedness and until it is accomplished we remain unhappy,
infinished beings.

God is always wanting to come closer to us, and in his
eyes the whole of our span of mortal life is meant to make
us accustomed to his nearness. God loves us and love is
always humble and respectful; it will not force itself upon
the beloved. God cannot love us to the full, that is, give full
scope to his love, be as lavish with us as he wishes, unless we
let him. If, from his side, our lives in this world are an opportunity for him gradually to give himself until we are capable
of receiving him fully, from our side they must be seen as a
response to his loving advances, allowing him to train and fit
us. There is never any question of the initiative lying with us or
of our having to get on the good side of God in order to win
his favours.

All that has gone before is an attempt to show how, in our
ordinary daily lives we should respond to God, surrendering to
his loving concern for us and his loving will to give himself. It
is not a part-time thing, it covers and must cover the whole
span of our lives. It is the beginning on earth of our life in
heaven. It is prayer : God incessantly giving himself, man
opening himself to this gift.

Jesus' whole life was prayer or, more truly, he himself is
prayer. In his own person he embodies God's gift to us and his
surrender to his Father. There is no other prayer but the
prayer of Jesus and real prayer is, of its very nature, a making

of his prayer our own. We have to identify with his prayer, surrendering with him to his Father and, in receiving him, placing our whole trust in him, receiving the Father's love. It is as if a great column of fragrant incense rose up continually from our earth – the prayer that is Jesus; we drop into the burning coals our own tiny grains and the wisp of smoke from them is mingled and absorbed in his.

Jesus has left with us a sacred rite whereby his perfect surrender to his Father, enacted all his life long, reaching its climax in his death, is concretised at a specific moment here for us; for us, precisely, so that we can deliberately, with most full intent make it our own. In the mass we have the deepest expression of what prayer is. Here God does everything. Here Jesus, his beloved, offers himself, the perfect offering of perfect love in which his Father delights. He delights in it because it gives him the supreme, eagerly desired opportunity to lavish himself on man. The reward of Jesus' surrender – and in what untold pain and darkness it was made and with what untold confidence and love – was God himself. Daily we have in our hands this perfect prayer as our very own.

We must make it more and more our own, and this means surrendering ourselves with his surrender so that we too might receive the Father's love to his heart's content. Again, this is not a part-time thing. Jesus' surrender to his Father was not a part-time thing, it was his very way of being, and so must it be with us. At mass, we renew over and over again our will to surrender with Jesus; from this sacrament flows the power of God to enable us to do so. It is the sacrament of union; every participation in it deepens our union with our Lord, a union which we must then live out in our everyday life. It is our very offerings, our bread and wine, fruits of our earth and works of our hands, that are transformed into the sacrifice of Jesus. What clearer message of the meaning of our work-a-day life?

If we want God, if we really long for union with him, then we shall want the mass with all the passion of our hearts. For some, daily mass will be possible and this most sacred act of prayer will sanctify their day. For others, only weekly attendance will be possible. It does not matter. If we assist with faith and desire it will transform our week. God is not limited by his sacraments; the efficacy of them far outstrips our categories, transcending space and time.

I have often heard it said that young people, and no doubt others who have not tried to understand its inner meaning, find mass boring, even distasteful. It is essentially the mystery of faith and nothing can substitute for faith. It cannot be interesting on the purely natural level but only when faith lights up the action from within. Undoubtedly everything must be done to ensure that the liturgy is carried out as perfectly and as beautifully as possible but everything must be at the service of faith. The ceremonial, the singing, everything must aim at illuminating the inner meaning of the mass and our share in it. Anything extraneous has no place in the celebration. To turn mass time into a sacred concert, or a prayer meeting, to make it too lively and interesting, with things to do and rollicking songs, is a disservice. It is substituting for the effort of faith. It is mere entertainment loosely connected with the mass, aimed at arousing emotion and keeping attention. One would want proper emotions to be aroused but only in the context of faith. At the same time, we must not be dependent on emotion and must be prepared to enter deeply into the mass whatever our feelings. Here too is the occasion for 'fast'.

If we really know what the mass is, we won't be too disturbed when things are not to our liking. Tastes differ and it will be impossible to please everyone. After all, we are celebrating sacrifice and it would be rather odd if, in the name of offering sacrifice, we insisted on having things our way and showed annoyance and resentment when our wishes were not considered. It is of the essence of our surrender to God that we surrender to our neighbour too; it is largely, almost entirely in surrendering to our neighbour that we surrender to God.

Therefore, at mass, consideration for our neighbour must have first place. It is essentially a communal act in which we must express our love and respect for our neighbour. The priest will have his idiosyncracies, people will cough and blow their noses, children will fidget and cry, music, translations may be in poor taste. This is a human situation, this is the place of sacrifice.

To opt out of this communal celebration, to elect one where we can be left to ourselves and our own devotions with a minimum of involvement, is to be self-indulgent, seeking our own satisfaction instead of the pure love of God and our neighbour. It shows too that we misunderstand the nature of prayer. We are seeing it in terms of what we do, how we feel, what we can achieve, how concentrated and recollected we can be. Whereas it is what God does that matters, and so long as we are open, intending to unite ourselves to Jesus in what he is doing and receiving from his Father, he can in fact do everything he wants to do in us. This is what matters. The very annoyances of the communal celebration can become matter for self-sacrifice. To spend the time at mass with our feelings outraged and yet to go on willing to be patient and loving so as to please God, can mean that we are closely united to our Lord. We may feel most unsatisfactory, feel that we haven't assisted well and been very distracted. All that is seeming. In God's sight we have been there for him.

Our reception of holy communion is saying 'Amen' to what Jesus is doing and 'Amen' to his summons to us to enter into his saving death. He will give us understanding of this death, showing us how it is to be fulfilled in our daily life. Only he can show us.

Much the same can be said of the sacrament of reconciliation or confession. Here the encounter with the saviour is focussed on forgiveness of sin, the recognition and public acknowledgment that we have sinned and that only in Jesus can we be reconciled with the Father and with our brethren. It is not merely the opportunity for us to express frequently, ver-

bally, our sorrow for our lack of love, our selfishness and care-
lessness, but actually to receive our Lord's own sorrow for sin
and his perfect atonement. Only he can really understand how
closed and unloving we are; only he can do something about
it. This sacrament makes plain to us that our own trifling
sorrow and efforts at atonement get us nowhere; they are of
value only when caught up in the column of loving worship
rising on earth from the heart of Jesus.

Is there anything less satisfying on the human level than
frequent confession? It demands perhaps a greater effort of
faith than does the mass. The presence and action of Jesus
is most deeply hidden. We feel that we can never do justice
in words to what ever we ourselves understand of our shod-
diness, still less to what it is in reality. But of course we don't
have to. God sees our heart. All that matters is faith in Jesus,
a coming to him for his knowledge, his sorrow, his atonement.
We are happy then at the poverty of our own sentiments. We
can be sure that when we come time and time again to this
sacrament, with what we see and what we don't see of our
selfishness, our Lord is able to work in us, purifying and healing us, every bit as powerfully as when he bade the palsied
man arise and summoned Lazarus from the tomb.

Sorrow for sin is not an emotion and need not, though it
may be, accompanied by emotion. It consists in a determination to do what we can to change, and surely one of its chief
manifestations will be the desire to approach the sacrament
given us for the purpose. To neglect it seems to indicate a lack
of seriousness in regard to sin. Sorrow is not remorse. Remorse
torments and worries; it occupies us with ourselves and para-
lyses life. In reality it is an escape. Occupied with it we don't
have to bend all our energies to trying to change or trying to
love here and now. Sorrow is trustful and refuses to dramatise.
Remorse has more to do with having let ourselves down, of
having lost our integrity rather than with having grieved God
and our neighbour. Sorrow has all to do with God.

The sacrament of reconciliation highlights for us our responsibility for others. We do not live for ourselves alone. How we live our lives affects the whole family, not on the level that we can perceive but on the deepest level of being. Our lack of love wounds the church, hinders her sanctification; our love hastens it. We come to the sacrament to repair the wrong we have done in the only way we can, that is, by opening the gates to the saving love of Jesus. The whole church is sanctified by our reception of the sacrament.

Jesus, and his disciples after him, takes for granted that besides liturgical prayer, prayer in the assemblies and in the family group, those who are his will pray in the secret of their heart. They will go into their own room, away from the attention and stimulation of others, to pray to their Father in secret. It follows the logic of love. We have a Father, a lover, we want to commune with him at the deepest level of our being. Of its essence, this communing is solitary. Though it does not demand physical solitude, it must be there whenever we are praying with others, at mass or in other gatherings.

However, Jesus showed us that deep communion with God demands time set aside exclusively for him, just to be there for him. It is like going into the desert for a space, perhaps a very brief space. There are forms of prayer in which we are consciously and deliberately aware of others, communing with God through them, but these forms must not be allowed to substitute for the more exacting, less satisfying, solitary communion with God. For anyone who loves God this does not need saying; their heart will prompt them, urge them to this. The time given may not be long but it will be given faithfully, daily. It will be seen as a duty of love, regardless of feelings or dispositions. Unless we are prepared to give this time, we cannot hope to achieve any depth of communion either at mass or other communal prayer. The liturgy provides me with things to say and things to do; unless I have this inner communion they can lack depth for me and keep me on the level of sense. Ideally the mass itself provides moments for this desert prayer. If we cannot take the trouble to give God a little unoccupied time, not prepared to 'waste' a little time on him, we cannot expect to live out our days for him.

This desert prayer calls for great faith. It has simply no meaning in this world, not even the meaning of a get-together in a highly spiritualising action such as the mass – as some might regard it. Our other good works, the activities of the day in which, as they are his will, we are open to receive him, yet carry within themselves their own *raison d'être*; desert prayer does not. As far as this world is concerned it is dead loss. What is more, it is not likely to be satisfying and for this reason too it can seem a waste – 'if I could do it well then it would not seem a waste', we might think – and tests our faith and love the more. There is nothing in the gospels to suggest that prayer is going to be delightful and satisfying. On the contrary, our Lord suggests the opposite. It is going to be hard to persevere and easy to grow faint. It will be secret from ourselves. Only one is going to be appreciative and get something out of it and that is God. He is going to repay us for something that is costly, for something that does not carry within it an immediate reward of satisfaction. If we try for that, well, he says, you have your reward.

Everything will depend on our having a correct idea of the nature of prayer, how it is God who works and we who receive. This will make us wise and we shall know how to pray. There will be no problem. If we understand this basic principle, why so many fidgets? Why so many requests for instruction? Prayer is going to be a very simple thing, so simple in fact that it may well scandalise us and dash our hopes. We wanted it to be an exalting, satisfying experience; after all, it is the highest activity of man! Once we have separated prayer and life, once we see prayer only as one function in life no matter how important, then we are really only after a technique, a skill. Prayer is self-surrender to God at every moment; the reality of our prayer will be the reality of our self-surrender, not how we feel, what we experience, the lights we get and so forth. Prayer is necessarily hard because self-surrender is hard.

G

How are we to spend our time with God in the desert? The answer is by being there with him, ready to receive him. This is the core; anything we think or say, whatever device we seize hold of to hold our attention so that we can give that attention to him, is simply to keep us there, surrendered to him, and therefore one device is as good as another.

Can one give specific directions? I am loathe to do so, aware as I am of the dangers of being told what to do. What *we* do then becomes the important thing, not what God does; we can make what we have been told to do our excuse for not being present to God. Prayer can become artificial – how easily. Instead of being there for God, as we are, just as we are, with nothing to cover up our inadequacies, our pathetic nakedness, we begin to deck ourselves out, to become important in our own eyes, to flirt with God, trying to win him by our arts and wiles. He needs no winning. He only wants the chance to be good to us and that depends on our reality. If we are dodging behind this and that, pretending to be other than we are, trying to achieve sentiments we don't have, trying to reach elevated thoughts, then we are not there, we have put a puppet in our place, and God cannot give himself to unreality.

We go before God as we are. This means we suffer ourselves. We accept feeling our total inadequacy, that we 'can't pray', that our thoughts wander, that we are earthy and unspiritual, more interested in the breakfast to come than in God. If we are upset and worried in an obsessional way, we go before him like that; if we are feeling angry and resentful we go before him like that. Of all our activities this desert prayer is the one where we are most likely to see ourselves as we are and to experience our utter destitution in God's sight. Hence its enormous value. It will be proof of our love to go on giving that time to God in which we see nothing in ourselves but poverty. This means we offer that poverty to God, spread it out before him.

The devices we use, if use them we do to maintain ourselves

in God's presence, will vary according to temperament and spiritual education. I knew of an elderly lady suffering from cancer. When she could not sleep she would creep downstairs and go to the room where the statue of the Sacred Heart was enthroned, a lamp burning before it. Here she would sit, hour after hour. Her daughter, hearing her, would come to see if she was all right. 'Go back to bed, Mary,' she would gently say, 'there is nothing you can do to help me, I am all right.' She could have prayed in bed but it helped her to have a focus for her prayer, and a well-loved image with its associations provided it. What matter its poor quality. She could see beyond it and commune with our Lord, drawing strength from his heart for her own passion and death.

Another, whose way of loving God had been through her loving care for her family and others, and whose way of praying was simply reciting vocal prayers and, during her housework, pondering over her family and their various needs and commending them and others to God, as she grew very old and could no longer work or see to read, took to saying the rosary. Whenever she was alone, and of course it was often, the rosary would be between her fingers. She had no pretensions as regards her prayer. She never felt she could pray the rosary 'well' and was only too glad when someone would come in and keep her company. If someone, coming in and finding her with her eyes closed and the beads in her hands, was quietly leaving, she would call them back. She was, like Mary of Bethany, doing what she could. The time she had to herself she was determined should be given to our Lord and the device she used was the rosary. What mattered to God was the intention of the heart, the direction of herself to him. Neither of these women had read a book on prayer or heard a conference but they had lost nothing. For others, of a more complicated, sceptical turn of mind, these ways might not appeal at all and they would find some other device more suited to them if they felt the need.

We cannot do better than base ourselves on the gospel.

Every word of it, every incident is for us; it is God speaking to us. Once we really grasp this we know how to pray. We are the leper asking to be cured, the sick woman clutching his garment, the blind man, the woman at the well; we are the prodigal running home to the arms of his father. This does not mean that we must actually take these incidents and use them in our prayer, but that constant reflection on them reveals to us the one with whom we have to do, what he asks of us and how we must respond. It is a very authentic approach based on truth.

There can be no conflict between prayer and work; if there is it is because we have wrong notions of prayer. To fret because we haven't a lot of time for silent prayer and the little time we have is in an unquiet atmosphere, or at a time when we are tired and don't feel like praying, shows that we are more concerned with what we get out of it than with pleasing God. The idea that we must have periods of great solitude in order to develop our 'spiritual life' is likewise mistaken. We might benefit by a period of rest, change and reflection in a quiet retreat but this is just a human need and nothing specifically to do with our growth in love. We might grow more rapidly in love by getting on with our ordinary duties, giving ourselves to others, and this will most certainly be the case if our desire for solitude puts a greater burden on others.

If we say we haven't time for prayer it may well mean that we don't want to take the trouble and make the effort. We always find time for what we have set our hearts on. At this point I feel embarrassed; what right have I to make suggestions to others in a vocation different from mine? If it is not presumptuous – and I feel it is – may I suggest how it could work out in a family situation? Both parents are busy all day, and the evening must be devoted to the family. How chilling, how wrong, for mum and dad to opt out because they want to go to church and pray! Still, perhaps the last half-hour before bed-time (after all, it could merely mean they retire a little earlier and who could find fault with that), mum and dad go off to their room to pray, to give the last half-hour to God. There will be times when this is impossible, when there is a party or a night out. If they really care, this would be foreseen and perhaps they could get up a little earlier the morning before.

A thoughtful woman said to me a little while ago that being a good catholic meant you could not live an ordinary life. She knew well enough that Jesus means us to live ordinary lives and this was a criticism springing from a wounded heart, not so much on her own account as on that of others whom she loved and who had suffered through wrong conceptions. I have been at pains to stress that holiness lies precisely in the ordinary; it does not call for the bizarre, the exaggerated and odd. On the other hand we must beware of falling into the trap of playing down the demands of love. We can be very good, and many people are very good, but this is not the same thing as belonging wholly to God, and if we want to belong wholly to God then we have to be very generous. If we want to belong wholly to God we must make sacrifices which in no way conflict with our loving duties to others, to give time to prayer.

12

Called to be holy

What is holiness? The question is crucial. Holiness is not something I can acquire. In the scriptures God is 'holy' and this term was used in an effort to express his transcendence, his inmost being, his own world utterly separate from the world of men. It means God's own, unutterable existence. A human being is holy insofar as he has come into contact with divine holiness. For this, the divine holiness must have drawn near and touched him, for man, of himself, cannot enter the divine ambience. God's life is inaccessible to him. To be holy in the absolute sense means that a human being has been taken right into this ambience, that he lives with God, in God's own sphere. The writers of the New Testament speak of christians as God's holy people; they are the saints, the holy ones. This means that they are so in calling; the whole meaning of their vocation as christians is to be drawn into the inmost heart of God. They are drawn in in Jesus who has made them his own. It is he, of humankind, who is the holy one absolutely, for he belongs completely to God; besides being on our side he is also fully on God's side. By our union with Jesus we too can enter, and do enter into God's holy world.

Holy in principle we have to become so in reality, we have to allow God to come close to us and by his closeness make us like him and able to live wholly in his sphere, his 'eternal life'. The divine initiative cannot be overstressed. Too easily we think of holiness as something we acquire. We do not acquire it but we must labour to prepare for God's coming to us and work with him when he draws near.

It is as if God endows us with wing structure. We have to work the muscles of these embryonic wings to make them develop but no matter how much we try, we cannot get off the ground, that is, away from self. When the wings, through exercise, are sufficiently grown, then comes a divine influence, a wind, that not only uplifts us but something of its strength penetrates the wings themselves so we can begin to fly, leaving self behind first from time to time, then for longer periods. Thus eventually we are in the painful condition of not being wholly in self and yet not belonging wholly to God. We are still within the influence of the earth, pulled back by gravity even though we are moving towards God. If we are faithful there will come a moment when God will stoop down, catch hold of us and sweep us up to himself, taking us right away from earth (self), so definitively that its power over us is lost for ever; there is no return. Henceforth we live with and in God. His powers, not our own, control all our activities. No effort of ours can achieve it. It is he himself who must snatch us away from ourselves.

All this sounds very exciting we might think, and we wish it would happen to us! Contrary to all expectations, though, for God to draw near to us, sinful as we are, means that we suffer. We read of instances in the Old Testament when God made himself known in some way to a man or woman. The effect was awesome dread, painful yet irresistible. When we read of such experiences, experiences of the numinous as we say, we might think 'that is very nice'; we would gladly bear the pain. But what we do not realise is that these stories are a pictorial image of *inner* experience, an experience that does not happen on the level of sense; sense which we think would exult in the living God even as it trembled with delicious fear.

For God to draw near means he comes at a level below conscious, sensible experience; his contact is with our deepest self and escapes cognition. Nevertheless, our inmost self is smitten, wounded by the contact, and the experience of this is anything but thrilling. There is not one element of it that will gratify us. It is a profound undoing, wrought within the prosaic, unromantic context of workaday existence. There is no visit to the gates of heaven, no rapturous embrace by the numinous, but ordinary life going on denuded of whatever spiritual acquisitions we thought we had. It is the very secrecy, the hidden character of this denuding that is all-important. If it is something we can be pleased with it quite obviously is not God, but another glittering spiritual toy we hold within our hand.

Stress God's initiative we must, but at the same time we must stress the need of most generous effort and cooperation. We must work out our salvation in fear and trembling, there can be no sitting back and taking it easy when we are in the context of loving service. Our lamps must always be burning and our loins girt, everything in us on the watch. This is the hard part – the doing our utmost and then having to count it as nothing, not merely in word (this is easy enough, we can all *say* we are unprofitable servants), but in fact. We must accept experience of the reality. We have to be prepared to let it all drop, counting it as dross, a very hard thing to do, yet this is precisely what is asked as God draws near; this is the denudation that must take place insofar as he is allowed to come close to us.

God has given each of us the task of fashioning a beautiful vase for him which we must carry up the mountain in order to place in his hands. This vase represents everything we can do to please God, our good works, our prayers, our efforts to grow to maturity; all this God values most highly. Into the making of this vase, then, we put all we have, our whole self. It is for God we are fashioning it, we tell ourselves. When it is finished we begin our journey up the mountain.

When we reach the top a double shock awaits us. God is not there – there is silence, no response when we make our arrival known. Secondly, the vase . . . it isn't beautiful any more. There it is in our hands, a tawdry, common pot . . . the vase into which we had put our all. A deep instinct is telling us that if we want God we have to go over the other side of the mountain and one glance reveals a steep, mist-bound, featureless face. We can't go down there with anything in our hands; we must drop the vase, still precious though so disappointing. We must drop it even if it has lost none of its lustre. Beautiful or not, we cannot take it with us, we must go to God with nothing in our hands.

Our spiritual achievement is our most precious treasure. It has to go. 'For his sake', cries one who understood this, 'I have suffered the loss of all things and count them as refuse, in order that I may gain Christ and be found in him not having a righteousness of my own, based on law, but that which is through faith in Christ' (Phil 4 : 8–9). Now we can only begin to see the shabbiness of all we have done and do when God shows it to us. But what matters is that we recognise that it is God who is showing it to us and gladly let it go. The ideas we had formed of God, our working plan of him, so to speak, is destroyed. 'Our' God disappears. It is only when he does disappear that we can meet the true God, who is mystery, and who leaves us baffled, wretched, bitterly aware of our lack of goodness. We thought we were doing well, we thought we were virtuous, we thought we were spiritual and look at us now, after all these years . . . Our minds wander at prayer, we have no light, no comforting, reassuring feelings which tell us that everything is well with us and that God is pleased. On the contrary we feel the opposite. Instead of going forward – our own idea of going forward – we seem to be going backwards. We are humbled to the dust and in danger of packing up unless we know what trust in God means. And, of course, since this painful condition is the effect of God's drawing near, faith and trust are infused. We are able to trust him.

It is what is meant by the infusion of divine strength. It isn't a bit exciting but is rather a pathetic, miserable experience on the conscious level. Ultimately we are faced with a choice : Are we going to trust God and leave ourselves? Are we going to make that blind leap in the dark which relies on the divine arms being there to catch us? Are we prepared to sacrifice our own self-satisfaction, our own inner assurances, and be willing for God to have what he wants regardless of what we want? Our beautiful vase must be dropped. We said we were making it for God and not for ourselves. Here is the test of whether that is true or not.

Now it is the sad fact that many, if not most spiritual people refuse this act of surrender. They do not accept the divine impulse and thus never leave the ground of self. They do not give God the opportunity of catching them up to himself; even his first, tentative approaches are rejected because they cost too much, and in the most sensitive area of all, where I feel myself to be safe, good, spiritually successful. The danger of this refusal is far greater among what we might call professionals – priests, religious, and lay people who are bent on 'living a spiritual life' – than among ordinary lay people who see themselves modestly trying to be good christians, trying to please God. Only too easily we substitute the 'spiritual life' or the 'contemplative life' for God. Without realising it we are intent on a self-culture. The proof is that, when God would take this out of our hands, and ask us to begin to live for him and not for our spiritual satisfaction, we refuse. God puts up with these twisted motives for as long as necessary but, if we have good will, he will try to change our direction. How passionately we cling on in the name of God.

Love seeks nothing for self, has abandoned all desire for self-satisfaction and self-importance. It wants God and God alone to be important. What we can do, what we cannot do; what we feel, what we do not feel, all this is irrelevant. If for him to be our own dear God, drawing us to his heart in Jesus, means in actual experience feeling the opposite, feeling that we are losing him, are disregarded by him then we are happy. He is good. We can trust him. This is humility and this is love, miles away from laziness and indifference which doesn't care enough to be upset. 'All this palaver about prayer and states of prayer; all this spiritual cultivation and narcissism. I have no patience with it. Drop it and get on with living'. So say I provided I do live, provided my whole life is witnessing to the fact that God is my all. A great deal of sloth can lie behind this plea for the simple approach.

What is called for is a tremendous act of faith and love and these will carry us to God. We can be sure God is infusing strength for the flight. But by and large we don't take the risk. We are like the man in the parable who hid his talent with the excuse that his master was a hard man who would be angry and exact vengeance if he failed; not one who could be expected to be generous. We aren't going to wager anything on God's goodness; we prefer to keep our precious talent, something we can actually see, like the vase, wrapped up in a napkin. After all, if we lost it, what a mess we would be in; what would we have to give to God? What a dreadful thing to come before him with nothing to show! Oh, how blind and foolish we are!

This undermining of our spiritual self-confidence so that we can really learn what it is to trust God is absolutely essential. Only God can do it for us, like the parent bird pulling the nest to pieces under its young to force it to fly. We keep replacing the fabric. We crave for spiritual security, or rather the feeling of security; real security is what God wants us to have and that can only be when we have let go our own securities, which are illusory, and rely on him alone.

The craving for spiritual guidance may well form one of these illusory securities. We want to be assured that what is happening in our prayer is all right, we want to be given definite guidelines so that we can feel safe. 'Direction', as already hinted, can be dangerous. For one thing it presumes not only an intimate knowledge of the one concerned but also a knowledge of God and his mysterious ways on the part of the director. Friendly advice on the basis of equality is one thing, to put one's soul in the hands of someone else is another. Many people have come into the catholic church or have gladly stayed in her because she represented security in this insecure world, with her incontrovertible authority. Now that this authority is being questioned they are upset and resentful. They have to ask themselves if they are not more concerned with feeling safe than with loving God.

A priest might have devoted himself to work for the poor. Everyone praises him for his selfless dedication – nothing is too much trouble, nothing too irksome. Then perhaps he is asked to take charge of a well-to-do, stick-in-the-mud parish, and he objects. The reasons brought forward will be edifying because he must convince himself that he is a man of God, but the real reason is that to work in such a parish will rob him of his sense of doing something worth while, something heroic; it would be a spiritual come-down and would tarnish his image of himself. It may be precisely in the non-glamorous situation of an ordinary middle-class atmosphere that the greatest generosity is called for, but probably it won't feel like generosity.

Again, someone might be given the choice between two offices, one of very high status, the other not, yet it is in the latter that they are most needed. Instinctively, at that depth where our egotism and the voice of God meet one another, they will know that in the latter situation they are likely to meet with frustrations and lack of appreciation, the rubs and set-downs that will shake them off their pedestal. God asks, the ego warns and the ego wins. Choice is made for the high position and specious, edifying reasons are given, deceiving the self. The real reason is the desire to be spiritually great. Isolated in the high position there is the opportunity to live a 'deep spiritual life' and shine in one's own eyes and in the eyes of others. All spiritual authority carries within it the danger of unreality, a pretence to ourselves and others that we are other than we are. Few, very few can accept high office and remain unchanged, refusing to assume a greater spirituality, a greater wisdom than they really have.

In one way or another we are eager to evade reality, the poverty of our human condition, and spiritual leaders as often as not encourage us in this. Very much was written at the time of the canonisation of Thérèse of Lisieux about sanctity being found in the ordinary ways of life, but have we taken it to heart? Recently an Arab hermit, Sharbel Makhlouf, was canonised. There was an article in one of the catholic papers commenting on his life as framed in the process. The very things which were held before our eyes for admiration, imitation and proof of his sanctity were precisely the excessive fast, long vigils, and detachment from his mother, whom he left weeping outside, refusing to see her when she came to see him! Where in the gospels can we find justification for this sort of thing? Who says these things have anything to do with sanctity? Not our Lord certainly. At best they are human eccentricities and not to be admired or imitated.

We need to remember that canonisation tells us no more than that we can be confident that this person is saved. It does not tell us that they attained holiness, that is perfect union with God, before they died. Who are the subjects of canonisation? Apart from martyrs, almost invariably celibates, founders of religious orders, religious, priests, ecstatics, hermits. Would Thomas More have been noticed were it not for his martyrdom? Almost certainly not; a married man who admits simply that he needs to be married; a man who loved his family and a cultured, rich human life; a man who expressed ordinary emotions. The church's deep aversion to sex still persists underground. No one who enjoys sexual intercourse can possibly be holy – good, perhaps, but not holy. It is not said in so many words but the attitude is there. Who can shatter this falsity?

Would Thérèse herself have been noticed, so simple and ordinary her life, were it not for the intense campaigning of her strong-minded sisters? It is doubtful, and proof of this is in the fact that, of all the passages from her writings that could have been chosen for her liturgical office, one is selected that is out of character; a passage expressive of high feeling, of burning desires for martyrdom, longing to fulfil every vocation; a grandiose exclamation quite at variance with Thérèse's ordinary state. What is more, Thérèse herself was distressed when her sister, Marie seized on it – how naturally! – to prove that Thérèse was different, oh, so different from others, including herself. Thérèse passionately corrects this wrong impression. No importance is to be attached to her fervent feelings, her desire for martyrdom; it is not these that matter, it is not these that make Thérèse pleasing to God. These are spiritual riches. What pleases God, what is her only real treasure is her awareness and love of her poverty, and her blind trust in God. But we don't take her seriously and, in our folly, select this grandiose passage as expressive of Thérèse's sanctity.

Would the pure life of Soeur Marie Bernard of Nevers have been noticed were it not that the young Bernadette Soubirous had been the recipient and bearer of a supernatural message? It is doubtful. She often shocked her entourage by her ordinariness. I have a picture of her as a postulant, a passionate, full-lipped, sensuous woman determined to pay the full price for God. On the back is a prayer referring to her as a 'meek and innocent child'. We cannot put sanctity where it belongs, right in the heart of humanness, in the mundane and earthy.

Spiritual pretentiousness and lack of truth is one of the greatest obstacles to holiness, for it is essentially self-seeking. One can pick up many a biography where in spite of the author's zeal to reveal the supposed sanctity of his subject, this untruthfulness peeps through. The 'saint' is secretly posing, playing to the audience; saying the 'holy' thing, reacting in a 'holy' way; occupied with himself and not with God. One touch of this and it has to be said there is no holiness there. What is impressive in Thérèse of Lisieux and Bernadette of Lourdes is their truth. They did not try to impress, they remained themselves and cared nothing whether others thought them holy or not. Possibly Thérèse, by temperament and upbringing, was liable to this showing-off but she met the danger head-on and resisted it. Bernadette was too straightforward even to feel the temptation. A good example in Thérèse's life is her refusal to follow the community fashion of self-inflicted physical mortification, considered then a requisite of true holiness (apparently it still is). Thérèse quietly but adamantly went her own way. She looked at our Lord and learnt from him. Anyone aware of the pressures current in an enclosed community will know what this meant in terms of courage and trust; self-doubt was bound to torment her, but this had to be answered with trust in Jesus.

Those who are really holy or are steadily moving towards holiness, live abandoned to God, seeking him and not themselves. This means in practice that they accept a life of mystery and insecurity; the ideas they have formed of God and his ways are turned upside down, nothing makes sense; all seems meaningless and what spiritual life they thought they had disappears. To themselves they seem no different from those who, with regard to God, live casually. Far from seeing themselves growing in insight and closeness to God, the opposite happens. Nevertheless they go on, pursuing their path, relying blindly on God even though he seems not to be there. They are beset by weaknesses of all kinds and fail to make a good show in their own estimation. All they do seems paltry and shabby, even their sufferings are not worthy of the name. They have nothing to fall back on, nothing within themselves to assure them that all is well, nothing except the one thing which is everything – faith in God's goodness and fidelity. They are willing to take the risk of trusting that all is well, that it makes sense simply because God is good and is their Father.

They are willing to take the risk, leap into the dark – that is what faith means. They lay the whole burden of themselves, how they stand with God, their 'spiritual life', on God, sure that he will never let them down; all their attention and all their energies are bent on doing his will, trying to please him. They abandon all care of themselves, all desire to see that they are making progress, all desire to be safe. They do not ask for any pat on the back, any echo of applause, any glimpse of their 'beauty'. They are not interested, they are interested only in God having what he wants. They are sure that he will always guide them, showing them how to please him at every moment, and that if there is anything in them that displeases him he will show them how to work with him for its destruction. They go on peacefully in their daily routine, feeling mediocre, unworthy of God, just like the rest of men. There is no posing, no pretension, they stand in the truth. Can we not see that not only has everything they have been given to God but also their very self? God alone matters. This is to be holy.

Holiness implies a deep knowledge of God. It is union with God, a union of love, and love always means knowledge. Scripture over and over again testifies to this profound knowledge of God in those who are close to him. No longer servants but friends; Jesus' own knowledge of his Father is communicated to them; they are no longer dependent on signs and figures, parables, but can receive a direct revelation emanating from his presence. It does not imply 'insights'; it is at a level below the conscious mind. What can be conceptualised is not it but may be an effect of it. It is as with a vast, deep lake, clasped and hidden in the bosom of a mountain. No one would know of its presence save the mountain which holds it were it not for the streams breaking through the mountain-side and cascading down into the valleys. From the deep inner source of knowledge light is shed on individual data; what is understood can be verbalised. However, the knowledge itself is beyond conceptualisation; it is not of things, even holy things, but of God himself. It is one thing with union. It is the wisdom Paul speaks of, a communication of the Spirit of God who alone knows the depths of God. It is this Spirit who enlightens Jesus, revealing to him the mind of the Father, and Jesus' mind is ours.

There is a certainty in this knowledge; the person knows he knows and can speak with authority. As Paul goes on to say, he is not subject to judgment by his fellow-men because they have not received such communication and simply cannot stand on the same platform with him. But surely to talk like this is to give everyone who fancies himself as a spiritual man the right to set himself up as an authority, and what happens then? What about authority in the church? Jesus himself answers on behalf of those who share his mind most intimately: 'As I hear, I judge; and my judgment is just because I seek not my own will but the will of him who sent me . . . I do not receive glory from men' (Jn 5 : 30, 41). Someone united to God cannot seek himself and this ensures the truth. Any communication of knowledge is completely disinterested and at the Father's bidding. If there is the slightest self-seeking, the slightest desire for the applause of men, truth suffers. The true friend of Jesus will only be saying what Jesus is saying and this means what the church is really saying, hidden as it not infrequently is within a lot of untruth. Because it is the message of Jesus it is not likely to receive a better welcome than when it was first delivered. It is more likely that those who come in their own name, who preach a doctrine more flattering to the human ego, will receive a better hearing.

I made a garden for God.
No, do not misunderstand me
It was not on some lovely estate or even in a pretty suburb.
I made a garden for God
in the slum of my heart :
a sunless space between grimy walls
the reek of cabbage water in the air
refuse strewn on the cracked asphalt –
the ground of my garden !
This was where I laboured
night and day
over the long years
in dismal smog and cold –
there was nothing to show for my toil.

H

Like a child I could have pretended :
my slum transformed . . .
an oasis of flowers and graceful trees
how pleasant to work in such a garden !
I could have lost heart
and neglected my garden
to do something else for God.
But I was making a garden for God
not for myself
for his delight not mine
and so I worked on in the slum of my heart.
Was he concerned with my garden ?
Did he see my labour and tears ?
I never saw him looking
never felt him there
Yet I knew (though it felt as if I did not know)
that he was there with me
waiting . . .
He has come into his garden
Is it beautiful at last ?
Are there flowers and perfumes ?
I do not know
the garden is not mine but his –
God asked only for my little space
to be prepared and given.
This is 'garden' for him
and my joy is full.

13

On earth as in heaven

Do many attain holiness in this life? We have Jesus' answer that few find the straight road to life; and holiness is life, eternal life with the Father here in this world. To be virtuous, very virtuous does not, of itself, mean holiness. The human ego, coveting its own security and glory, can build a magnificent palace of virtue. A holy person will also be virtuous, but it will be in the way our Lord was. Those who secretly seek their own glory will follow a pattern of virtuous living, an accepted pattern and be deeply concerned not to depart from it. Hence their narrow-mindedness, their lack of flexibility and freedom. The holy person will not be concerned with patterns, but every moment will be looking to our Lord to learn how to live. They may well depart from the accepted pattern and thus others may fail to recognise their holiness. It seems to me that this will usually be the case, as with St Thomas More, St Thérèse and St Bernadette. But as Jesus' friend cares nothing for himself this does not weigh with him at all. He isn't interested.

Although it seems that few find the road to perfect union within the span of their life-time, some do find it before they die, at the end of that span. Old age with its 'undoing', as well as illness, can prove an effective instrument in God's hands with which to complete his purifying work. I have witnessed two instances where I am confident, certain in fact, that it was so. Both were women, one a nun, the other a lay woman.

The first, the nun, was a woman of generosity and integrity but of a neurotic disposition which increased as the years went by. She simply could not trust. She craved, with a passion I have rarely seen, for spiritual security. Perfect observance of the rule, self-control, these mattered intensely. When she could get along well with these she was happy but at the same time rather smug and inclined to be censorious of others. Mercifully her temperament upset her little boat at every turn. She would be going along splendidly and then, without warning, a sudden squall would overturn her. She couldn't forgive herself for her lapses, hated herself for the jealous, angry, resentful feelings that swept over her; she was plunged in misery. She had a friend in the community who tried to get her to see the meaning of it all; how our Lord in his love wouldn't allow her to grow smug. What seemed to her a dreadful affliction was, in fact, her chief blessing. Thus it went on, brief periods when she felt fine, had the tiller and controls in her hand, quite pleased with herself, able to put the painful awareness of her true condition to the back of her mind, then suddenly the sky would darken, the storm break loose and over she would go.

It was only about a year before she died that the penny began to drop and she to see in a real way what trust in God might mean. As always she struggled to respond. There was never a time, in all her painful life, when she did not try, when she was content to settle down. Our Lord wouldn't let her settle down; she would have liked to have felt beautiful and good. Our Lord listens to our deepest self and its wishes and he knew that she really wanted him more than her own security, and he answered that wish in this painful way. Then she became ill and within three weeks she was dead.

She knew she was going to die. She asked her friend to visit her each day. The latter was embarrassed and disconcerted for, tucked up in bed, away from painful conflicts with others, aware that soon she was to die and yet not really feeling she was dying, her boat was placidly sailing along. For the time being she was choosing to forget her poverty but only for a time. Her deep self, just before the end, three days before in fact, rose to the occasion, or rather sank to the occasion. She let everything go; she was able to make the surrender she had not been able to make throughout her life, try though she would. Because she tried and never stopped trying in spite of most painful humiliations, our Lord was able to fulfil all her desires. She knew he had done so and communicated this knowledge to her friend. Everything was changed for her, not on the emotional level but on the level of being.

It is a mistake to think that nearness to death in itself brings enlightenment and conversion. If we have refused throughout our life to see the truth about ourselves we are not likely to accept the light at the end. Only those who have the habit of welcoming light will welcome it then. If we have insisted on posing during our life we are likely to pose even in that grave hour. If we have any doubt of this we should think of the proverbial Jack the highwayman, joking and quipping on the scaffold. Human beings are odd! If we have played a pious game with God all our life we are likely to play it to the end. The sister I have spoken of allowed herself to be detached from the security game she would like to have played.

The lay-woman was a person of great natural power and charm. All her long life she had struggled to overcome her bad tendencies and to serve God in every way she understood. Faith was dark for her; she did not feel any love for God and thus thought she did not love God, and this kept all pretension at bay. She is the woman of the rosary I have mentioned earlier. At the end of her long life she was serene, sweet, patient, prayerful. Could she go further in this life? She was still in possession of her self. Must God wait until after death for the final dispossession? For several years she had wanted to die, life had lost its savour. Yet her deepest self belied this wish. Her deepest self wanted God with a passion she could not register in her consciousness but which refused to allow her to succumb to death. Her deepest self knew she was not yet wholly God's and said 'no' to her wish to die.

Then she broke her hip and was snatched away for several weeks from the nest where she had been cherished with every care to the operating theatre and the hands of strangers. Suffering from shock, weak and helpless, for the first time in her life, probably, she was no longer in control of herself or the situation. She was not a domineering woman, she had no need to be, she was powerful by her sheer charm. Even when she was very old and frail she was still in control; but now was so no more. Her moorings were snapped, every landmark had disappeared and she was tossed rudderless on the waves. Fears and doubts that her buoyant, affirmative nature had kept down now surfaced. The hearts of those who loved her were torn but this was God's work of love and they knew it. So did she. In her confusion, beneath it all, she knew, and her habit of saying 'yes' to God enabled her to say it now. Eventually she was brought back to her nest, where after several weeks of suffering she died. The moment she was ready, the moment she was all his, she died. She 'died' before she died. This is the blessed privilege we should all covet and be prepared to sacrifice everything for. To die before we die is to change the nature of death; it is to die the death of Jesus and is, in its deepest reality, not death but assumption. Isn't this something of what the doctrine of Mary's assumption is trying tell us? If we let God have his way with us, death is truly overcome, we do not die; death is dead.

> And now no longer ours but yours
> Within your death we too have died,
> And rise to sing the Father's praise,
> Within your glory glorified.
> Liturgy of Holy Saturday

What if the work is not complete before physical death? When someone closes their eyes in death, when clinically it can be said this person is dead, from then on our vision is shut off. What is happening to that person remains shrouded in mystery for us. We have the certainty that great things are happening but what and how we know not.

We have some knowledge of what but are quite unable to imagine or concretise it in any way. The catholic instinct has always held on to the notion of purgatory; it has shrunk from the easy assumption that most people at death 'go straight to heaven'; a healthy realism keeps it in this position. It is true that revolting crudities have clustered round the kernal of truth and there is a sense in which we can deny the existence of purgatory if by that is meant the lurid and cruel caricatures of what is essentially an operation of the most tender mercy and love. To posit a purification after death is no insult to God's mercy nor to the power of redemption. Mercy, ever poured out in lavish flow, must be received. We have not allowed it to wash over us in life and, if we are to reach our perfect fulfilment and happiness in God, which is his dearest wish, then we must consent to be drowned in these purifying waters after death.

Both in life and after death, it is love that purifies. If in life we allow God to come close to us in love, to take us in his arms and hold us fast, this inevitably means pain, simply because we are so twisted, hard, and unyielding. If we submit, his love softens us, straightens us out, transforms us into his own likeness. The pain of purification is the direct effect of love. And this is the same after death. How it happens then we cannot know but we are certain it is love's last passionate plea for acceptance. Love's last throw, we might say. Presumably we can still say 'no' either entirely or in part. Confronted with the overwhelming love of God and with our own mean response, instead of grief melting our hearts and casting us sobbing into his arms, our pride can hold us back, like sulky children, still refusing to be loved.

The evangelist John corrects for us any distorted notions we might draw from the parabolic expressions of judgment and punishment in the synoptists. Parables are not allegories. The infuriated employer casting his servant into prison until he has paid the last farthing is not God; nor is the Lord who refuses to open the door to the late-comer. The parables aim at driving one point home; the build-up of character and incident serves that one point only. John shows us the true nature of judgment and punishment. 'We read our judgement in your face.' Jesus has come into the world as a light and everything is shown up for what it is against that light. In his light we see ourselves as we are. If in our mortal life we come to that light, allow it to judge us, do not evade its searing rays, and if we follow its path to the Father's heart, our judgement is already taking place. We allow ourselves to see him as he is and therefore become like him. All in us becomes him, becomes heaven.

On the contrary, if wholly or in part we refuse his light and chose to remain in darkness, it is not he who stands over us and condemns us, we condemn ourselves. We deliberately keep away from light and life and joy. He cannot transform us. When the veils are taken away and light shines with unbearable intensity we cannot but see ourselves as we really are. We judge ourselves because we see ourselves against his beauty and his love.

Anyone who reads the gospel with even minimum attention must be awed by the gravity with which our Lord warns us of the possibility of ruin, a ruin which is self-destruction. He stresses and stresses the seriousness of our lives, the lasting effect of every one of our choices. We are answerable for all. He was shocked and grieved at men's frivolity before the demands of life, which are the demands of God. Everlasting, ultimate ruin is possible. It is not that God cries out to us 'depart from me ye cursed into everlasting fire'. It is we who say to ourselves : 'I choose to live away from life and love; I choose to live in the hell of my selfish self.'

Can we conceive of a human being who has not one spark of goodness in him, who is mere smoking flax . . . but this, we are told, is precisely what Jesus will nurture and not put out. It might be no more than kindness to a bird or animal but in so far as it is goodness, in so far as it is human, it is truly godly, truly 'heaven' and heaven belongs to heaven. In Matthew's gospel the criterion of 'heaven' is goodness to our fellow-men, and of hell, neglect and unkindness. In his own way John says exactly the same; those who love the brethren, and in the measure that they love the brethren, pass from death to life.

Is it a case of some being summoned to the reward of heaven because of their charity and others banished to hell for their lack of it? Is it not rather that in each of us there is both heaven and hell in that there is some love and care for our neighbour as well as some lack of love? Who can say that he has always fed the hungry, covered the naked, ministered to the material, psychological and spiritual needs of his neighbour to the utmost of his power? If we could say that, then we would be all heaven, for heaven is where God is, it is his eternal life, his own intimate sphere of existence. Only that is in heaven which is transformed into God, nothing ungodly can enter there. At the same time is there anyone who has not rendered some service to his brethren?

True repentance in this life, which means a willingness to see our sin and the determination to change with God's help, can transform evil into good. Unrepented of, evil remains. We take it with us beyond death. Perhaps in the experience of death itself – who knows, perhaps after death – there is still opportunity for total repentance so that all in us becomes heaven. But presumably there can remain elements of hell within us for ever. Presumably it is possible never to achieve perfect fulfilment, never to give God the fullness of joy which could be his did we allow him to love us to his heart's content. Who can say that there is not grief in heaven, a grief that is not incompatible with happiness? He taught us what should be the heart of all prayer to the Father, the cry that his kingdom should come, his will be done on earth as it is in heaven. We are praying that everything in us be transformed into heaven whilst we are on earth so that at death we can enter triumphantly into our inheritance.

Can we say anything of that inheritance? It seems to me

that many people when they say they cannot believe in an after-life are saying that they have no way of thinking about it or imagining it. Surely this is inevitable. We have to send our loved ones into the dark and in our turn surrender to the darkness. We do not know, eye hath not seen, ear not heard, the heart of man is unable to conceive what it is like to live with God. We turn to Jesus, our brother. He tells us that our destiny is to be with him, where he is, and that reassures us. Moreover, that being with him where he is begins in this life and indeed, can reach completion in this life; eternal life, a reality in this our mortal span. During his life on earth he was always with his Father, in closest union with him, but because of his mortality the full, blissful effect of that union could not be experienced. It seems rather that, though being the source of unutterable confidence and joy, it was yet a suffering experience. He had to pass through death in order that God's closeness should transform his whole being, filling it with God's own bliss. So it is with us. We have to live with Jesus in the darkness, held close to his Father's heart, we have to consent to pass with him through the dissolution of death so as to receive ourselves again new-minted, freed for ever from every element of corruption, every particle of our being infused with the radiance and joy of God. It was for this we were created.

'Come, blessed of my Father, come receive the kingdom prepared for you before the world was made'.

Conclusion

Before bringing this book to an end I want to stress again an aspect of believing in Jesus which is of supreme importance and which is, perhaps, the least understood. This lack of understanding is productive of far-reaching, unhappy consequences for our growth in his love. What I am referring to is the truth that of ourselves we cannot die to self so as to live with Jesus' life. This death to self is essentially mystical, due that is to a direct contact of God. All efforts to induce this death only increase the strength of the tentacles we wind around ourselves to prevent our being carried off by God. It is God and God alone who can take us from ourselves. The death must be death 'in Jesus'.

Many religious teachers, both christian and otherwise, have aimed at training their followers to die to what is natural and human in themselves: every pleasure must be sacrificed and if it is unavoidably there then the mind must be diverted from it; our judgment, emotions, delight in the senses must all be denied for the sake of union with God. Only when we have transcended our sensual, bodily selves can we be united with God. This is false. It is probably true that nowadays few people push this to extremes but something of this attitude still governs their lives. There may be more leniency as regards bodily needs but still a rigid denial of psychological and intellectual ones. We end up barren virgins.

From this serious misconception springs in great part the rivalry, if we may call it that, between religious and secular life. The one is seen over against the other. Baleful consequences follow. Religious can easily find assurance (secret, unadverted to as often as not because their 'charity and humility' must tell them differently), in the fact that they have 'given up so much more' and 'do so much more' than other people. By the very fact of being religious they are a cut above the common man and very special to God. This illusion must be ruthlessly destroyed and the reaction of many to any attempt to destroy it is proof enough that it is an illusion. The 'glory' they take in this 'doing more', as they think, is wholly opposed to desire for God and is a clinging on to their own life in such a way that Jesus can never lead them into the depths of his death, which is true life.

On their part lay people look on and react in various ways. Some have a naïve approach. Religious are the salt of the earth, God's chosen ones; it is only they who can hope for real holiness, we others have to jog along as best we can, which is all God expects of us. After all, we have our families to look after, we can't give a lot of time to prayer. What is more, we have lots of pleasures and enjoyments and these disqualify us from holiness. We would have to renounce all these things and live odd, bizarre, subnormal human lives. At bottom, they really want to think this. It excuses them from generosity. They don't want to be faced with the truth that they too are called to holiness. They listen to this, now often repeated dictum, nod their heads in assent but don't take it seriously because they don't want to, and find their rational or semi-rational excuse in the above arguments.

Others take a hostile attitude. They feel a sinister challenge in the presence of religious life, especially the enclosed, contemplative form which seems so alien. Its functioning seems antithetical to their normal lives; can both be right? Can God ask all that of some? Is that the price one has to pay to belong to God? These more thoughtful people are sincerely bewildered; it doesn't make sense. They try to give themselves to God, they want him and all the while are uneasy. One or other side must be wrong and so they reject the idea of the 'bizarre' way of life. To accept it would seem to condemn their happiness in marriage, their interest in their work and career, the comforts of ordinary, comfortably off people, a tasteful home, nice food and so forth.

What we have to be thoroughly convinced of is that all that matters is God's will for *us*. What is he asking of us? Of one he asks this and of another he asks that, and it is foolish, a waste of time, an escape from devotion and wholeheartedness in our own vocation, to be looking over the garden fence at the green – or parched – grass on the other side. Each of us must have the deepest respect for God's will for the other. Even within the broad vocations of religious or lay life, each of us has his own quite special vocation and he must be allowed to fulfil it in freedom and honour. No one must demand that another go our way or be critical because his way differs from ours, or feel his way is an overt criticism of our own. There is a true sense in which each of us must challenge the other but only in the degree of generosity we live our lives.

While it is true that, of ourselves, we cannot die to ourselves, and God in no way wills unnecessary deprivations, but wants us to delight in the good things he has given us and grow to maturity through their proper use, nevertheless we have to deny ourselves. This means we have to renounce our selfishness relentlessly, always. We have always to be putting our duty and the welfare of others before our own pleasure and satisfaction. It is not deprivation for its own sake, it is a matter of love – loving God and our neighbour more than our own selfish interests. Most of us, both religious and lay people, are not generous enough.

A Carmelite, Poor Clare, Cistercian, Carthusian, whatever, can be thoroughly selfish even though they perform their duties regularly and would not be thought of as bad religious. Many can be just 'good monks or nuns' but nothing more. The austere practices, the very safeguards and the routines can become a snare. Nothing can substitute for personal dedication, an unremitting labour of love, one's eyes fixed on God all the time to see what he asks here and now. It is this generous endeavour, whether in religious life or in lay life, that enables God to work in us and effect that mystical death in which lies our blessedness.

If some religious, perhaps the minority nowadays, persist obstinately in giving God what he is not asking and expecting him to work miracles on their behalf when he offers them proper means of human development and wills them to take them, others have forgotten the special demands he makes of them. He does ask certain renunciations of religious which he does not ask of lay people and we fail him if we refuse them. Too easily nowadays, realising the falsity of past views, religious go to the other extreme and wrongly allow themselves what is wholly proper, indeed for lay people God's will, identifying with their way of life as the natural, christian one for all. Each of us must give what God asks of *us*.

Any thoughtful, honest person who is not concerned with their own security and therefore not on the defensive, could not think that the renunciations asked of religious are greater than those asked of lay people. They may be different but they are not more painful. Throughout my religious life it has been a sobering, helpful thought, when smarting under hardship and renunciation, to recall what is asked of people outside. There are sufferings and trials and bitter choices religious are never asked to bear or make. What harder than struggling on with a difficult marriage? We can never know the anguish of losing a life-partner, experiencing the illness and death of a child, the searing shame and frustration of not being able to provide adequately for the family, and the thousand and one sufferings and trials little and great that face men and women.

The evangelical counsels are for all, it is the way of carrying them out that differs. All are called to perfect chastity, the gift of self in truth and love; everything about us, our words, our bodily gestures, limpid, expressing what our hearts are saying, and these hearts pure with Jesus' purity. All of us must obey, putting others before ourselves, submitting ourselves for the good of all, wholly at the service of others, sacrificing what we want for what is best for all; accepting obedience to legitimate authority in an intelligent way, bowing before the inevitable. Each of us must possess some things, no one can void himself of everything, but whether we have little or much we must be detached, never making possessions our god, our security and confidence. We must be free, and generous with what we have, ready to feed the hungry and clothe the naked. Once again, the fact that religious have publicly vowed chastity, obedience and poverty and put themselves in a structure which reflects or signifies these values, can blind them to the implications and make them in reality far less chaste, obedient and poor than others.

It is not the degree of hardship or suffering that matters – God loathes our suffering – but the love with which we deal with it. Human life is hard and the more generously and lovingly each of us takes up the particular cross we have been given, the more we help one another. As long as life lasts, we must be strong, selfless and loving, full of concern for one another, making it easy for our brothers and sisters to love God and do his will. While we are forgetful of ourselves, even of our spiritual progress, for we are not concerned with living a spiritual life but with loving God, all the while our Love will be giving himself secretly at our furthest depth. Like the seed sown in the earth, the good earth well-prepared by rain and frost, by plough and harrow, and warmed by the sun, it will grow without our knowledge until the harvest has come.